Tony vK

LANs EXPLAINED
A Guide to Local Area Networks

LANs EXPLAINED
A Guide to Local
Area Networks

W. SCOTT CURRIE, B.Sc.(Hons) 1st class
Local Area Network Development Manager
Edinburgh University Computing Service

ELLIS HORWOOD LIMITED
Publishers · Chichester

Halsted Press: a division of
JOHN WILEY & SONS
New York · Chichester · Brisbane · Toronto

First published in 1988 by
ELLIS HORWOOD LIMITED
Market Cross House, Cooper Street,
Chichester, West Sussex, PO19 1EB, England
The publisher's colophon is reproduced from James Gillison's drawing of the ancient Market Cross, Chichester.

Distributors:

Australia and New Zealand:
JACARANDA WILEY LIMITED
GPO Box 859, Brisbane, Queensland 4001, Australia

Canada:
JOHN WILEY & SONS CANADA LIMITED
22 Worcester Road, Rexdale, Ontario, Canada

Europe and Africa:
JOHN WILEY & SONS LIMITED
Baffins Lane, Chichester, West Sussex, England

North and South America and the rest of the world:
Halsted Press: a division of
JOHN WILEY & SONS
605 Third Avenue, New York, NY 10158, USA

South-East Asia
JOHN WILEY & SONS (SEA) PTE LIMITED
37 Jalan Pemimpin # 05–04
Block B, Union Industrial Building, Singapore 2057

Indian Subcontinent
WILEY EASTERN LIMITED
4835/24 Ansari Road
Daryaganj, New Delhi 110002, India

© **1988 W. S. Currie/Ellis Horwood Limited**

British Library Cataloguing in Publication Data
Currie, W. Scott
LANs explained: a guide to local area networks. —
(Computer communications & networking).
1. Local area networks (Computer networks)
I. Title   II. Series
004.6'8   TK5105.7

Library of Congress Card No. 87–35284

ISBN 0–7458–0238–9 (Ellis Horwood Limited — Library Edn.)
ISBN 0–7458–0535–3 (Ellis Horwood Limited — Student Edn.)
ISBN 0–470–21063–X (Halsted Press)

Phototypeset in Times by Ellis Horwood Limited
Printed in Great Britain by Unwin Bros. of Woking

Contents

To
Bronwen, Pamela, Edward and Rosalind

Preface

The rate of development of Local Area Networks has been truly remarkable over the past few years, but the rapid appearance of new products, and equally rapid disappearance of some old products, has left many potential users confused and apprehensive about how to proceed.

LANs Explained is intended to introduce the concepts behind the major local area networks, principally to managers and technical staff who may be required to make purchasing decisions. It has been pitched at a level between a 'full blooded' technical text book and the sort of 'idiot's guide' usually produced by the manufacturers, which is, understandably, biased towards their view of the world.

The book is a direct result of a survey of LANs available in the UK, which I undertook for the Computing Service of Edinburgh University, at that time called Edinburgh Regional Computing Centre, and published under the title 'The LAN Jungle Book'. The many complimentary comments made about its introductory section, which is the briefest possible overview of LAN technology, encouraged me to think that a book such as this would be justified.

The final influence was the fact that the standards being promoted for LANs are now taking shape, and therefore one can predict with some confidence that the material included will still be relevant in years to come.

The layout of the book
The book is divided into five parts. The first part, the *Introduction*, covers definitions and the current state of the LAN market. It also introduces some of the technical jargon carried over from traditional wide area networking, and attempts to categorise LANs by what they can be used for.

The second part, *Technology*, examines first the various media which are employed for LANs and then introduces the generic topology and access techniques which are mostly unique to LANs. Throughout the first two parts various *Technical notes* are included at the end of some of the chapters. These give a more detailed explanation of some non-LAN-specific terms which the reader already familiar with communications may wish to skip.

The third part, *Architecture*, examines in some detail the three major LANs which have become the focus of the standardisation efforts, plus five of the most popular PC-LANs, i.e. LANs aimed solely at the PC market.

The five have been chosen both for the typical features which they exhibit and for their probable long term durability.

The fourth part, *Protocols and standards*, introduces the software which runs over LANs, and in particular the communications protocols (rules) which govern data interchange. The first section of the part deals with the International Standards Organisation standards for Open Systems Interconnection, and the second with other 'standards', including those which dominate the PC-LAN market.

The final part, *Futures*, encompasses the slightly peripheral aspects to LANs, namely extended LANs and network management. These, although very important, have lagged behind the development of LANs, and thus can fairly be described as 'future'. The final chapter attempts to predict likely developments in both hardware and software.

Acknowledgments

I would like to thank Peter Williams, deputy Director of the University of Edinburgh Computing Service, for his permission to use material gathered for the original survey mentioned above. The following, all members of the Computing Service, have also been of great assistance: John Murison, for his sterling efforts in reading both the first and second drafts; Chris Adie; John Henshall for his comments on Chapter 10; and Bill Byers for his on Chapter 11. I would also like to thank David Stewart-Robinson for access to the Apple MacIntosh and for his helpful comments on the format of the illustrations.

Extracts from BSI documents DD 98 (ISO DP 8802/3), DD 99 (ISO DP 8802/2), DD 100 (ISO DP 8802/4) and DD 136 (ISO DP 8802/5) are reproduced by permission of the British Standards Institution. Complete copies can be obtained from them at Linford Wood, Milton Keynes, MK14 6LE.

Finally my deepest thanks are to my wife, Bronwen, and children, Pamela, Edward and Rosalind, who had to endure the loss of my attention for far too long while I was producing the manuscript.

Part 1
Introduction

The introductory part of the book presents two ways of defining what is meant by a Local Area Network (LAN). The first is a formal definition of the characteristics of a LAN, and the second is a categorisation of LANs by examining the many uses to which they can be put.

The categorisation includes the use of traditional Wide Area Networking techniques, and many of the technical terms necessary to understand how LANs work are introduced.

1

Definitions and background

1.1 THE LOCAL AREA NETWORK MARKET

Local area networks have rapidly become the major growth area within the computing industry, and are widely expected to remain so until at least the early 1990s. A primary reason for this growth is that LANs are a critical element in Office Automation, a process which is expected to transform the lives of many working people in the future (Pape 1983).

A formal definition of a LAN is given below, but basically it is a system for linking computers over a limited area. In particular LANs are increasingly being used to connect Personal Computers (PCs) and thus their sales growth is related to that of PCs.

Several recent reports, for example in *PC-Week* (1986-A, 1986-B), indicate that there were around 20 million PCs in use at the end of 1986; this is expected to increase to 48 million by the late 1980s (Fig. 1.1). Only some 600 000 PCs (3%) were attached to LANs, but this was estimated to increase to 9%, 4.5 million by 1990. This acceleration of LAN attachments is confirmed in surveys of large US corporate users of PCs, reported in *PC-News* (1986), where respondents indicated a switch away from connecting PCs directly to mainframes, using for example 3270 emulation, towards LANs with *gate-ways* to the corporate mainframe networks.

A second major factor in the expected growth of LANs is the onward march of the same technology which enabled computing power to be distributed in the form of desktop PCs. This will affect LANs in two ways. First, the nature of PCs themselves is certain to change, in that by 1990 one can expect a machine operating at several MIPS (Million Instructions Per Second), with several megabytes of fast memory, to be on sale for the same price (or less) as today's PCs. These machines are available today, although at a high price, and fast communications will be essential.

Second, the cost effectiveness of VLSI technology (Very Large Scale Integration — the packing of vast number of components onto single silicon chips) will be applied directly to communications problems. In particular, most of the software which implements the *rules* by which computers agree to interchange information, i.e. to *protocol software*, will be held on chips, rather than occupying the host computer's memory and processor, and thus the cost of connecting a PC to a LAN should fall. This is already happening with the agreement between IBM and Texas Instruments on the provision of

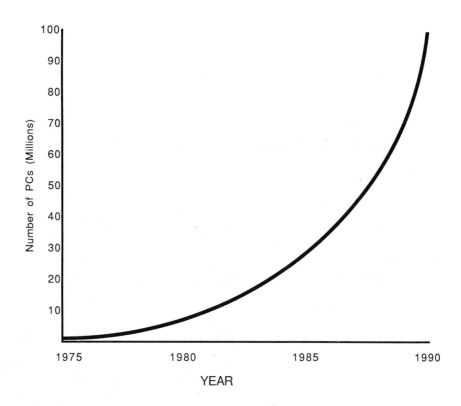

Fig. 1.1 — Estimated worldwide PC usage growth.

the chip set for the IBM Token Ring LAN. At present this comprises five chips, the most complex of which has 195 000 elements. Although they are expensive to design (Rudin 1986), one can expect such chips to become more readily available.

Finally, many software producers are now addressing *network appli-cations*, in particular distributed databases and electronic mail, which some predict will become as commonplace as the telephone in the business community. There is therefore a trend, particularly in the field of *office automation*, towards the installation of complete packaged systems, com-prising LAN hardware, workstations and software. It is therefore apparent that most companies, large and small, will have to examine LANs in some detail over the next few years, and it is the intention of this book to provide the basic background to the relevant issues, technical and otherwise.

As shown in Currie (1986), there are more than 400 different LANs and related products worldwide (or LANs with different names at least), and more than 130 competing for the UK market alone, with an estimated 12 000 LANs installed. Most of the installed LANs are very small, however, a typical average being eight stations (International Data Corporation 1986). This reflects an attitude on the part of purchasers towards trying out various options before too large a commitment is made. With such a volatile marketplace and rapidly changing technology, very few are willing to invest on a company-wide basis. One of the reasons for the diversity of LAN products is the very size of the potential market, plus the problem that each PC and mainframe manufacturer has adopted a different approach. Other reasons include the lack of well agreed standards, as well as the fact, which will become apparent in the 'technology' section of the book, that different requirements need different solutions, and the different technologies give opportunities for new approaches to traditional computer networking.

1.2   DEFINITION OF A LOCAL AREA NETWORK

One formal definition of a local area network is 'a transmission system intended primarily for linking computers and associated devices within a restricted geographical area'. As Chapter 2 will indicate, such a definition can be applied to many different systems, some of which can also handle other forms of communication — speech and video for example. The computing equipment involved may range from a full-scale mainframe system to various types of desk-top device incorporating microprocessors as well as terminals and peripherals.

An alternative way of defining a local area network is to list its major characteristics, as follows:

Area covered   The network is restricted to an area of moderate size, such as an office block, a factory, or a campus. The limiting factors are usually the overall length of the cable used and any interdevice restrictions imposed. In practice the distances involved range from a few metres to a few kilometres. A very few can cover tens of kilometres, but are still described as *local* networks.

Speed   The raw data transmission rate on the network is high (of the order of 1–100 Mbit/s) when compared with ordinary telecommunications circuits. Fig. 1.2 indicates the position of LANs relative to other forms of data networking.

Connectivity   On some LANs, particularly those associated with *Open systems* (see Chapter 10), every device on the network has the potential to communicate with every other device on the same network. In practice, many of the smaller LANs operate on a *master and slave* basis, with slave PCs clustered round a master shared filestore, and no direct slave PC to slave PC communication.

Cost   Relatively inexpensive methods are used to connect to the network, compared to the cost of the device being connected. This does not apply in all cases, however, as it is still expensive to connect a low cost station, such as an IBM-PC, to a 10 Mbit/s LAN.

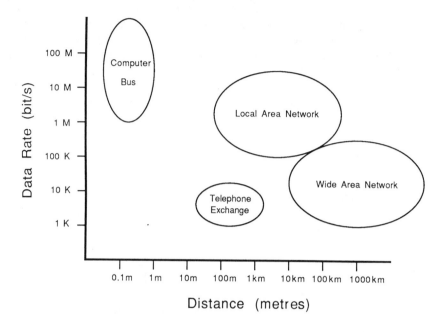

Fig. 1.2 — LANs relative to other networks.

Resource sharing   One of the fundamental features of most LANs is that the network is shared between the devices. Whereas on a traditional network each machine will be directly wired into a *switching* device (see 2.1), on a LAN the one physical medium is usually shared, along with access to the medium.

Low error rates   The errors introduced by the network are very few, when compared with traditional wide area networks.

1.3   ADVANTAGES AND DISADVANTAGES OF LANS

The technological advances which have produced distributed processing have already been mentioned. Prior to these developments, most computer users were served by *multi-user* systems on a central mainframe. Such a system had, and still has, several advantages in terms of sharing hardware and software resources: expensive peripherals, common data and software packages.

Local area networks have resulted from the attempt to provide the same levels of resource-sharing to the end user who has a personal computer on the desk. Thus LANs are designed to permit the interchange of data between machines and to allow access to shared resources, e.g. discs and printers.

Another role for LANs, which is developed in the next chapter, is to carry out the traditional networking task of connecting terminals to computers. Many LANs can combine this activity with the resource sharing one, and indeed some can provide telephone and video channels as well. Thus potential savings can be made by integrating all communications into the one system, although there is a corresponding risk of total disruption in the event of a network failure.

Several other potential advantages are also apparent. A distributed system of computers on a LAN is inherently more reliable than a central system, as the loss of any one machine should not impact significantly on the whole system. This is not the case on many Shared Disc LANs, however, and the loss of the LAN itself can be catastrophic.

One of the major potential gains provided by LANs is the ability to connect equipment from several vendors. In practice this depends on the software support either from the LAN supplier or the computer vendor, although the situation should improve with the increased implementation of standard protocol software.

There are also several potential organisational benefits. For example, one of the greatest expenses in the relocation of staff is often the rewiring necessary to provide communications. Once a company-wide LAN has been installed, however, and assuming that there has been sufficient forethought in the placing of access points, it should be possible to achieve a high degree of flexibility in the location of equipment. Another potential benefit is the possibility, applicable to some organisations, of regaining some control over the equipment purchased by departments, which in many cases is totally incompatible. The enforcement of conformance to LAN standards can have a stabilising effect, although some (James 1987) see this as the "old guard" of mainframe data processing managers trying to keep control of an organisation's computing power. On the other hand, the great flexibility of some LANs, and the potential of Open Systems can result in the opposite, i.e. departments buying many different types of computers, in the knowledge that they can simply plug into the LAN.

On the deficit side, the main problem at the moment is the lack of well defined standards in the field. Much of the work described in the chapters on protocol standards has still to be realised in products, and this may take some time. The distributed nature of a local area network also raises two other major problems. The first is Network Management, i.e. how to control access to the network, the measurement of performance and the prevention of the over-installation of equipment. Secondly there is the data security problem of keeping widely distributed information both private and valid, while maintaining multiple user access across the network. These and other problems are discussed in the later chapters of the book.

2

Categories of local area networks

There are many ways of dividing local area networks into categories, the most common being by technological differences, discussed in Part 2. It is instructive, however, to examine first the application of traditional computer networking techniques to local area situations, and then consider the different uses to which LANs can be put.

2.1 TRADITIONAL NETWORKING TECHNIQUES APPLIED AS LANS

There are two reasons for examining traditional computer networking in a book on LANs. First, many of the techniques and much of the jargon has been directly transferred to LANs, and these can be introduced at this point. This section is a concise introduction to the concepts; a much fuller account of general networking principles can be found in Deasington (1984). Second, traditional networking products may be applicable, often with greater cost effectiveness, in situations where a LAN solution appears at first glance to be the more appropriate. The manufacturers of these products often market traditional products as LANs, although they may not meet many of the criteria included in the definition of a LAN given in Chapter 1.

The fundamental concept in all computer networks is the *switching* of information from one station to another. A *station* is any device which can communicate, and the devices which enable communication to occur are usually called *nodes* or *switches*. In many LANs there are no switches as such, as the operation of the LAN itself performs the switching between the attached stations. The concept of switching had been around for many years before the advent of computers, for example in the telephone system, and three main switching techniques are well established: Circuit Switching, Message Switching and Packet Switching.

2.1.1 Circuit switching
Circuit switching is the technique of dedicating to the communication a physical path between the transmitter and the receiver, the path being termed the *circuit*. Communication requires three phases, setting up the circuit, transferring the data and closing down the circuit.

Fig. 2.1 shows a typical multi-node (switch) network with several

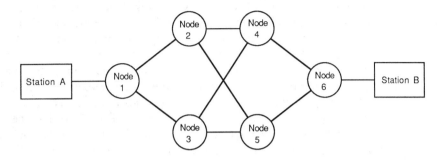

Fig. 2.1 — Typical multi-node network.

attached stations. For station A to transfer data to station B it must ask its nearest node, in this case node 1, to set up a circuit to station B. Station B is identified by an *address,* normally a unique number, just as every telephone has a unique number. Node 1 will choose the next leg of the route, say to node 3, and so on until station B is reached. The choice of routes will probably depend on the level of node traffic and possibly the cost, but once established will be fixed for the duration of the call. During the data transfer stage each piece of information follows the same route, and that route is reserved for that circuit. Note, however, that each internode route will normally be *multiplexed,* i.e. shared between all the circuits currently open between the two nodes. Multiplexing techniques are the subject of a Technical Note at the end of Chapter 4. The pieces of information are normally individual characters, plus any other signals which are relevant, for example, indications of being ready to receive data. At the end of the data transfer, or *call,* the circuit will be cleared down through each node.

The essential point about circuit switched networks is that once the circuit has been established, neither station should be able to detect any difference between the networked connection and a direct physical cable between the two stations. These networks are commonly used to provide connections between terminals and individual computer ports, although the most common example is the telephone network. Their use as LANs is discussed below.

2.1.2 Message and packet switching

The two main alternatives to circuit switching involve the grouping of data into units, followed by the transmission of those units, one by one, to the destination station.

In *message switching* there is no dedicated path, but the transmitter *appends* the address of the destination station to a complete unit of information, called a message, and transmits it on the network. These units can be very large, and each is completely independent of any other. Each switching node on the network will look at the address and decide how to get the message to its destination. This is much more efficient than circuit switching, which can waste lines by keeping them open when no data are being transferred, but introduces considerable delays in switching, and requires nodes with sufficient capacity to store complete messages.

Another advantage of message switching over circuit switching is that the receiver need not be ready to receive when the transmitter wishes to send—indeed there is no direct communication between the two stations at all. Station A (refer to Fig. 2.1) simply sends the message to node 1 and 'forgets' about it, although it may receive a delivery acknowledgment later. Node 1 will pass the message on, and if station B is unable to accept it then its nearest node will normally store the message until it is able to do so. The most common use for this type of network is in military message systems and telex-style networks.

Packet switching is an attempt to compromise between message switching and circuit switching, and it comes in two flavours: *datagram* and *virtual circuit*. In both kinds the whole message is split up into smaller messages, called *packets,* which will typically be under 1 Kbyte long. In a datagram network, each packet is treated like a message in a message switching network, i.e. no circuit is needed and each datagram travels independently to its destination. The major difference is that the datagrams are related to one another in that they have a specific sequence and thus form a larger message, or they may be part of a 'terminal-to-computer' interactive conversation. On large networks with many nodes this can result in packets arriving out of sequence, and consequently the software in the station can be complex. However, the technique is well tried in, for example, the U.S. Defense Advanced Research Project Agency Network (ARPANET).

The other approach is to set up a *logical* circuit, called a *virtual circuit,* between the transmitter and the receiver, down which the small packets can be sent. The circuit is logical in that no dedicated physical circuit is kept open for the call—it is simply an agreement between the two stations and any intervening switches that a circuit exists between them. The three phases of calling are the same as in a circuit switch. Establishing a call ensures that the receiver is ready to listen and in some cases negotiation can take place as to how quickly data can be sent. In most virtual circuit networks, each packet follows the route of the previous one, i.e. each node does not have to decide where to route each packet as it does in a datagram network. All that each node has to do is record in tables which logical connections are passing through it, and thus where each incoming packet must be sent next. This gives greater control over the sequencing of packets, recovering from the loss of packets during transmission, and controlling the flow of packets: for example if the receiver gets busy it can restrict the number of incoming packets.

Virtual circuit techniques, of which probably the most famous example is the X.25 protocol, impose a smaller processing load on the nodes and stations and are generally better for long exchanges of information. Datagram networks are more reliable, as the loss of a node does not imply the loss of the circuit, and work well for shorter interchanges. Most local area networks are based on packet switching, as packets are transmitted by the end stations, but using the LAN itself as the switching node. In many cases the LAN itself is inherently a datagram network, although virtual circuit services are also offered to the stations. This is reflected in the discussion on protocols and standardisation in Part 4.

2.1.3   Circuit switches and PABXs as LANs

Digital circuit switches are designed to switch digital signals in the same way as the telephone exchange switches analogue signals (see Technical Note 1). A detailed discussion of the techniques used to implement digital switches is beyond the scope of this book, but may be found in Stallings (1984).

The problem which digital switches traditionally address is that of connecting terminals to host ports without directly wiring the terminal to the port. The solution is to wire the terminal and the host ports to a switch and let the terminal user select the port required (Fig. 2.2). Normally the switch will distinguish between terminal and host ports, but some switches will permit general interconnection between all the ports, and so can be used, for example, for PC-to-PC communications.

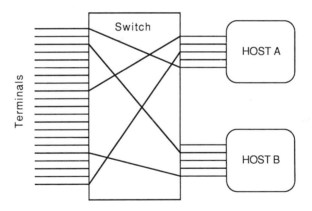

Fig. 2.2 — Data circuit switch.

The major disadvantages of this approach is that all the terminals must be wired to the switch and the provision of many host ports can be very expensive. For a large mainframe, it is often more cost effective to provide a packet network interface, e.g. X.25, which can support many simultaneous calls, than to provide the same number of individual ports, although some switches now offer the facilities of packet networks discussed below. The second disadvantage is the lack of character buffering between stations, which means that the caller and receiver must be transmitting and receiving at the same speed.

Digital switches come in a great variety of sizes, from 8 ports to thousands of ports, on one physical switch or on a network of switches. They can be very cost effective and should be compared against LANs, particularly the wiring replacement LANs of 2.2.2, as a solution to the 'terminal-to-host' problem mentioned above.

A special case of the digital circuit switch is the PABX (Private Automatic Branch Exchange), most instances of which can now offer data switching as well as the switching of telephone messages. They are sometimes referred to as Computerised Branch Exchanges (CBX). A schematic of a typical wiring installation is shown in Fig. 2.3.

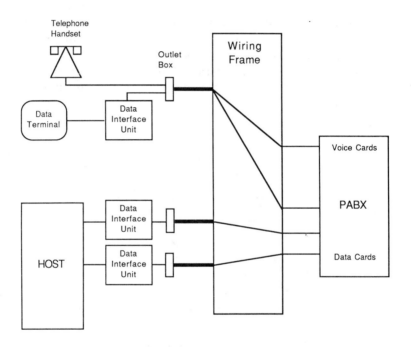

Fig. 2.3 — Typical PABX wiring schematic.

The wiring to the outlet is usually three-pair, two wires being used for the telephone, two for data, one ground and one spare. The pairs are twisted together in a sheathed cable and are separated out at a wiring frame near the exchange. The telephone wires are connected to one type of exchange equipment and the data wires to another. These systems are designed to switch a 64 Kbit/s stream of digital data, which is the standard for digitised voice. Unfortunately, digital telephones have not yet progressed far beyond the development laboratory, and are very expensive, so the voice data is analogue as far as the exchange, where it is digitised. In the foreseeable future there will be digitised telephones, which should simplify the exchange equipment.

On the data side, there are very few 64 Kbit/s terminals on the market, and so a Data Interface Unit (DIU) is required to encode the data traffic onto the 64 Kbit/s stream. These can be very expensive, and as there are no standards yet for this encoding each manufacturer uses a proprietary system. One recent report, (Berman 1986), estimates the cost of adding a data port to a 'voice and data' PABX as roughly twice that of adding a similar port to a 'data only' circuit switch. The 64 Kbit/s streams are synchronous (see Technical Note 2 at the end of the chapter), and the exchanges can handle synchronous or asynchronous data.

The main advantage of using a PABX as a LAN is that a building only has to be wired once, and so the customer has only one supplier to deal with for the purchase and maintenance of the total system. The main disadvantages, apart from the cost of data ports, are the possibility of data traffic interfering with voice traffic, by overloading the PABX for example, and the data speed restriction of 64 Kbit/s. PABXs are designed to cope with telephone traffic, and a careful balance must be achieved between the number of data ports, which must support calls of long duration, and the number of telephone ports, which must support many more calls of relatively short duration. While the speed limit of 64 Kbit/s may seem more than adequate for today's terminals, it may not be sufficient for the networking of graphics terminals, laser printers and video disc filestores which we can expect to be required in the near future. A more detailed discussion of the use of PABXs for data can be found in Gilmore (1985).

The final variant on using telephone wiring for data traffic is a system called *Data Over Voice* (DOV). This can utilise a six wire system, similar to Fig. 2.3, but using a separate 'data only' switch alongside the PABX. A more common DOV technique is to take advantage of the unused bandwidth of the two voice wires to transmit the data *above* the voice, i.e. at a higher frequency on the same cable, but still separated out to two different switches. Usually only asynchronous transmission at speeds of up to 19.2 Kbit/s is offered.

2.1.4   Packet switches as LANs

Packet switching networks are very common in Wide Area Networking, and can be used as LANs, particularly on a campus sized LAN. Apart from the nodes, which are usually linked by high speed synchronous lines, the network requires some form of terminal concentrator or PAD (Packet Assembler/Disassembler) to provide the interface to the terminal or host. This is shown in Fig. 2.4. Typical examples are the Department of Defense Advanced Research Project Agency (ARPA) network in the USA, which is datagram based, and the British Telecom Packet Switched Service (PSS) in the UK, which is based on the X.25 virtual circuit protocols.

The advantages of this approach are the relatively low cost, in that even a PAD can normally be used as a stand-alone node for a few ports, and the immediate availability of well proven products. While synchronous data can be handled at moderate speeds directly into the nodes, the PADs usually offer only limited speed interfaces.

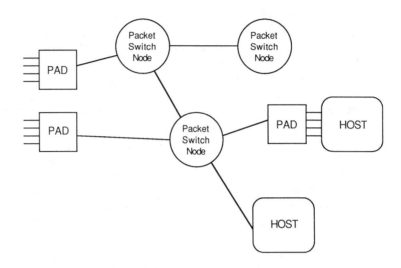

Fig. 2.4 — A packet switched network.

2.2 CATEGORISATION OF LANS BY USAGE

By examining market surveys, such as Currie (1986), one can draw some broad conclusions as to the uses intended for the various LANs by their manufacturers. The approximate percentages in each category are shown in Fig. 2.5. Note that the numbers are the percentage of the total of 140 or so different products on the UK market which fall within each category; they are *not* an indication of market share.

2.2.1 Small filestore LANs

Approximately 13% of the LANs on the market are targeted at linking a very few, usually 4 or 5, personal computers together. They are not strictly LANs, as they rely on the fact that most PCs, and in particular the IBM PC, have a few V-24 (RS-232) ports which are not normally used. Thus a configuration such as shown in Fig. 2.6 can easily be established.

The essence of the small filestore LAN is that the central PC or filestore has total control over the LAN, i.e. it operates as a *master* with the other stations being *slaves*. The slave stations are configured such that a part of the central filestore, normally a hard disc, appears as an extra disc drive to the slave, possibly with a shared area by means of which files can be transferred between the slave PCs. One or more printers on the central PC can also be shared, but there is no direct transfer of information between the slave stations. The system works by modifying the PC's operating system to allow the networking tasks to be performed in *background mode,* i.e. without interfering with whatever the PC user is doing. Small filestore LANs are aimed at single offices or very small organisations and usually offer only limited speeds and distances from the shared PC.

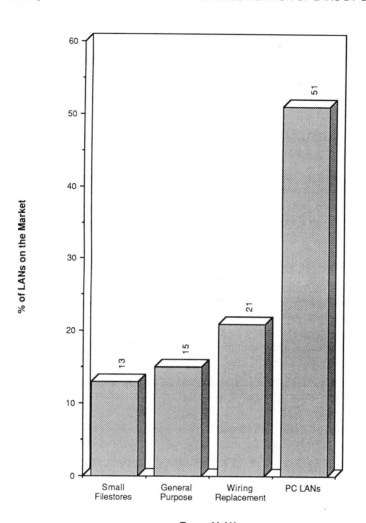

Fig. 2.5 — Distribution of LANs by type.

In terms of user facilities they are equivalent to *multi-user mini computers,* where one processor drives several terminals. Multi-user minis can be much cheaper than small LANs, mainly because only simple terminals are required for each user, and less technical expertise may be necessary to maintain the system. Some more sophisticated systems use remote processors to give the illusion of a LAN. These systems suffer, of course, from having a single point of failure, i.e. if the central processor fails no-one can work, but the usefulness of having a working PC on an inoperative LAN may also be limited. The choice between the two approaches depends on the applications being run, and the desire of possible long term expansion, which may be easier with a carefully chosen LAN.

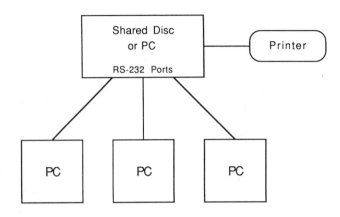

Fig. 2.6 — A small filestore LAN.

With wordprocessing and spreadsheet applications, where the main load is between user and screen, a LAN should be more efficient, whereas constant access to a large database may be better dealt with on a multi-user mini.

2.2.2 Wiring replacement LANs
Some LANs, other than the switches discussed above, also primarily address the 'terminal-to-host' problem. The main selling point of these LANs, apart from offering potentially greater speeds, is the saving which results from having a single wire running round a building, rather than radial wiring from each terminal to the switch. Overall, some 21% of all LANs are marketed in this way, but they can be divided into two distinct types.

At the low cost end, wiring replacement LANs typically offer a 9600 bit/s asynchronous interface for up to 255 stations, with the LAN itself running at 500 Kbit/s or less. There will be some limit to performance, in that only a few dozen full speed connections will be supported at any one time, but the cost can be very low, below £200 per port typically. At the other extreme, some networks based upon high speed LAN technology, such as *Ethernet* (Chapter 7), are supplied with PAD type boxes which provide various interfaces; this is discussed further in 2.3. The suppliers restrict access to the LAN itself, usually because some proprietary protocol is being used, and hence such LANs are in the wiring replacement class. Because of the high speed of the LAN, such systems will support many simultaneous connections and offer thousands of ports. They also offer the possibility of adding stations directly to the LAN in the future, if the set of protocols used on the LAN can be matched in the station.

2.2.3 Personal computer networks
The Personal Computer LAN, sometimes referred to as a *microlan,* is essentially an extended version of the small filestore LANs. In this case, however, there is a physical LAN medium with one or more shared file or disc servers, and usually with each PC's discs and printer being shared with

others on the network. The networks vary in size from a few dozen to many hundreds of PCs. The major difference between these LANs and the wiring replacement LANs is that a board within the PC is used to provide the attachment to the LAN. The board will commonly handle all of the networking protocol required, thus relieving the PC proper from this load.

PC LANs are discussed in some detail in later chapters as they constitute just over one half of all the LANs on the market. Some 19% of all LANs are aimed solely at the IBM-PC, with a further 19% handling the IBM-PC plus at least one other type of PC. The remaining PC LANs (13% of all LANs) are not capable of dealing with the IBM-PC, and are largely the PC manufacturer's 'own-brand' LAN. The important role of the IBM-PC and its software as a standardisation force is examined in Chapter 13.

2.2.4   High Speed LANs
High speed LANs are a specialist development for mainframe-to-mainframe communications over small distances (e.g. within machine rooms) operating at high data rates, typically 50 Mbit/s. They are intended to provide high speed access to computer room peripherals, e.g. discs, and between mainframes. Most work in this area has been done in the USA—indeed only Network Systems Corporation's Hyperchannel is easily available in the UK. They are not discussed further in this book.

2.2.5   General purpose LANs
Finally we are left with general purpose LANs, whose aim is to permit heterogeneous equipment from different manufacturers to communicate. The equipment can range from large mainframes and minis, through PCs to 'dumb' terminals. It is these LANs, of which the best known are the IEEE 802.3 CSMA/CD (Ethernet) and the IBM Token Ring, which have received most attention from the standardisation committees, and indeed many computer science purists would claim that these are, under a strict definition, the only permissible LANs.

Owing to their considerable importance, the later sections on standards, protocols and specific architecture concentrate on these LANs. Note, however, that they represent about 15% only of the LANs on the market, although this can be expected to grow considerably in the next few years.

2.3   LAN SPEEDS AND DEVICE INTERFACING
There are two other aspects of LANs which are worth considering in general before examining the intricacies of LAN technology, namely the speeds at which LANs work, and how terminals and computers are interfaced to LANs.

2.3.1   LAN speeds
The raw speed at which a LAN operates mainly affects the number of simultaneous connections which it can support, rather than greatly raising the delivered data rate at an individual station. In practice the very fast

LANs can be a serious embarrassment to a relatively slow station, in that the time taken to process a packet from the LAN can be much greater than the theoretical inter-packet gap time. This in turn means that even on LANs with very low inherent error rates many packets can be lost by the stations themselves being unable to react in time to the arrival of several packets.

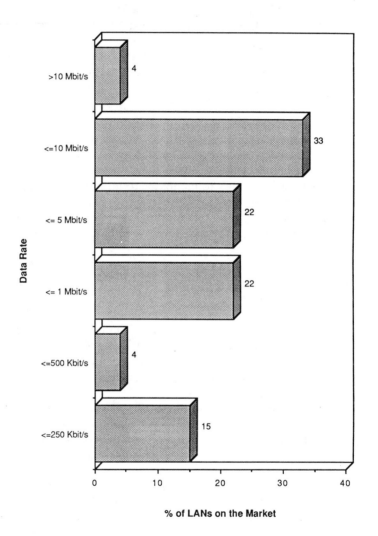

Fig. 2.7 — Distribution of LANs by data rate.

The spread of raw LAN speeds on offer is shown in Fig. 2.7. Those at the lower end of the spectrum are often the wiring replacement type or the small filestore LANs. Note when choosing a PC LAN that, although the raw speed may be adequate for normal use, it may be unsatisfactory when performing occasional tasks, such as the downloading of many PCs with the same package from a central filestore at the start of the day, or at the start of a tutorial session in a classroom.

2.3.2   Interfacing to the LAN

There are two basic approaches to interfacing to a Local Area Network, both illustrated in Fig. 2.8. The first is for the LAN manufacturer to produce a Network Interface Unit (NIU), sometimes called a Bus Interface Unit (BIU), which presents a number of standard computer interfaces to the outside world. Typically these will be RS-232 (V-24) or IEEE 488 ports, and they enable almost any PC, terminal or peripheral to be attached. A simple program, which can be totally independent of how the LAN itself works, can then be used by a PC attached to an NIU to gain access. Mainframe computers can also be attached by using direct links from the computer's terminal ports to the NIU ports, or in some cases the NIU will emulate a standard wide area networking protocol, such as X.25 or IBM 3270.

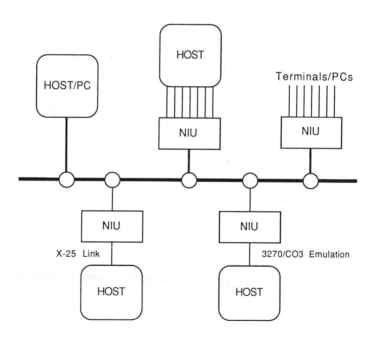

Fig. 2.8 — LAN interfacing techniques.

The second approach is to provide a card which connects the PC or larger host directly to the LAN, by plugging into the host's internal bus. The card may have all of the LAN software on board, or may require extensive software on the host, but this method is likely to be more efficient and is potentially cheaper for a large host.

Both of the above solutions can be expensive, however, particularly for the faster LANs, and they emphasise connecting either 'dumb' terminals or the existing ranges of PCs. LANs were initially developed, particularly by Xerox, to link together very powerful processors, which would not have any local disc storage and would therefore require very fast networks to access remote discs. Current workstations which connect directly to LANs usually have a local hard disc, and are thus expensive, but a few manufacturers are researching low cost discless workstations. Thus one can envisage several types of interface to a LAN, from the expensive workstation through the range of cheaper PCs and the directly connected terminal to the simple terminal attached via a Network Interface Unit.

Finally, when LANs are considered for a particular application, the maximum number of devices which can be attached must be borne in mind. This can be difficult, as some manufacturers quote the number of NIUs or directly connected stations, and some quote the total number of ports. Fig. 2.9 shows the range in the number of direct connections permissible, with 255 being a major dividing line.

Technical note 1: Analogue and digital

The major difference between current telephone networks and computer networks is that the telephone system is mostly *analogue,* at least from the handset to the exchange, although it may be *digital* between exchanges. The words 'analogue' and 'digital' can cause great confusion, as they can be applied to the transmission techniques, the signals, or the data being transmitted.

Analogue data, for example voice or video, takes continuous values over some measuring interval, whereas digital data takes discrete values, usually reduced to binary 1s and 0s in the computer world.

Analogue signals, i.e. the means of propagating information, are continuously varying, whereas digital signals again take discrete values, usually two voltage levels, one representing binary '1' and the other binary '0'.

Analogue transmission is the sending of data over some medium, usually a wire, by the use of analogue signals. Digital transmission uses digital signals over similar media.

Both analogue and digital data can be represented by either digital or analogue signals. Digital data can be represented by analogue signals by using a *modem* (modulator/demodulator). The most common example of this is the use of dial-up lines over the telephone network. Similarly,

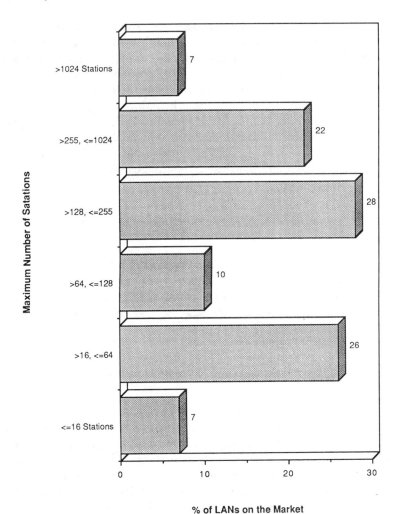

Fig. 2.9 — Distribution of LANs by stations.

analogue data can be converted to digital signals by using a *codec* (coder-decoder).

Analogue and digital signals both require some form of regeneration from time to time, in order to extend the distance covered by a network. Analogue signals are regenerated by *amplifiers,* but these will also regenerate any noise the signal has picked up. Digital signals are regenerated by *repeaters,* which, because only two discrete signal levels are involved, can produce a clean signal. Analogue signals, however, can travel further than digital ones before regeneration is needed, and thus analogue networks can cover much larger areas than digital networks. Analogue networks form the basis of broadband LANs (Chapter 4). The various techniques for extending digital LANs are discussed in Chapter 15.

Technical note 2: Asynchronous and synchronous transmission

Asynchronous transmission is the sending of individual characters, usually encoded as 8 bits, each preceded by a *start bit* and followed by one or two *stop bits,* as illustrated in Fig. 2.10. Between characters the transmitter sends continuous stop bits, which have value 1, and the receiver knows that a character has started when the start bit, which has value 0, arrives. The gap between characters can be of any length—hence the term 'asynchronous'. Most micros and dumb terminals use asynchronous transmission out of the ubiquitous RS-232 port, and thus most LANs will offer asynchronous ports even if the LAN internally uses synchronous transmission.

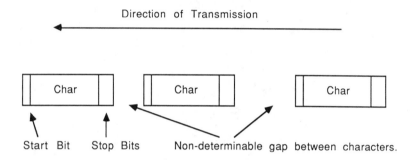

Fig. 2.10 — Asynchronous transmission.

Synchronous transmission is effectively *packet* transmission: blocks of characters are sent with a *start code* of synchronising characters (the SYNC character) before each block, and a few *stop* characters after the block (Fig. 2.11). Each block is called a *frame* and this form of transmission requires that the transmitter and receiver each have a clock. The two clocks must be synchronised, either by a separate clock line or by some technique of embedding the clocking in the data. Some terminals, e.g. ICL's CO3 terminals, and many networks, both local and wide area, use synchronous transmission as it is more efficient and can support much higher transmission speeds.

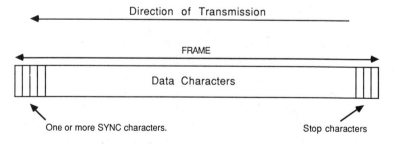

Fig. 2.11 — Synchronous transmission.

Part 2
Technology

This part deals with the four main technological aspects of concern when discussing LANs: the transmission medium, the topology, the transmission technique and the station access method.

The four aspects interact in various ways, for example some access methods are only suitable for some topologies or with certain transmission techniques.

The techniques described also provide a convenient classification scheme for describing LANs.

3

LAN media

The first technological aspect to be considered when discussing local area networks is the *transmission medium*, the nature of the physical path along which the data must travel. This is related to the other technical factors such as the topology and access control methods (discussed in subsequent chapters), as some media are only suitable for certain topologies and access methods, and vice versa. The medium can also limit the raw data transfer rate of the LAN.

There are three main media in use in LANs, *twisted pair* cable, *coaxial* cable and *fibre optic* cable, Fig. 3.1 shows the percentages of LANs on the market which use these media; it can be seen that coaxial is by far the most prominent.

Before these media are examined separately, the reader is referred to Technical Note 3 at the end of the chapter, which explains the terms *bandwidth* and *attenuation*.

3.1 TWISTED PAIR

For general networking the most common transmission medium is *twisted pair* cable. It is the most common because it is used for the telephone network to link each handset to its local exchange, and indeed is often called *telephone wire*.

Each circuit requires two insulated wires, which are usually made of copper and twisted together in a helical pattern. Multiple pairs are commonly bundled together into one cable, and the twisting of the individual pairs reduces the possibility of *crosstalk* (interference between the pairs), as well as lowering their susceptibility to interference from external sources. There are many such sources of interference, ranging from heavy industrial plant to fluorescent lights and photocopiers. This twisted pair technique was discovered very early in telephony and holds good for data transmissions, whether analogue or digital, at low frequencies.

The technique of *shielding* is also used to reduce interference. This is the wrapping of a protective sheath of strong material (usually a metal braid) around the twisted pair cable, which can improve the resistance to interference by a factor of 1000 or more (Bates & Abramson 1986). Shielding is especially important for data transmission at higher speeds, as the suscepti-

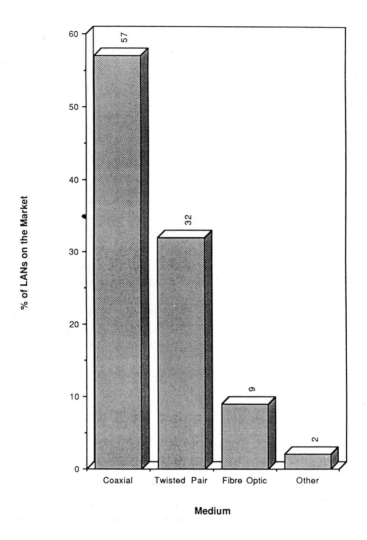

Fig. 3.1 — Distribution of LANs by transmission medium.

bility to crosstalk increases exponentially with the frequency of the signal. It enables fast data rates to be transmitted further without regeneration, although the distances possible are shorter than with most other media.

Twisted pair, which has the additional advantage of being easy to install, requiring little specialised skill, is being used very successfully in local area networks, notably in Cambridge Ring networks, which run at up to 10 Mbit/s over shielded twisted pair. IBM have also standardised on twisted pair for their cabling system, offering both shielded and unshielded, depending on the user's requirements. Their shielded twisted pair consists of a core of two twisted pairs of copper wire, each in a plastic sheath, wrapped around by aluminium foil and copper braid, and then enclosed in a second plastic sheath. This form of wiring derives great strength from the braid but is rather more expensive than normal twisted pair. However, it has the capacity to carry data up to 16 Mbit/s.

In general twisted pair is suitable for limited distances in environments where there is little possibility of external interference. It is the cheapest of the three principal media.

3.2 COAXIAL CABLE

Coaxial cable is probably the most versatile for LANs, offering high speeds over moderate distances at moderate prices. It is therefore, as Fig. 3.1 shows, the most popular LAN transmission medium. Like twisted pair, coaxial cable comprises two wires, but its design of a single inner conductor and a hollow outer conductor (Fig. 3.2), with insulating material between,

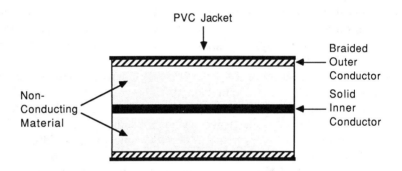

Fig. 3.2 — Construction of coaxial cable.

enables it to have higher bandwidth and work at higher data rates than twisted pair.

There are two types of coaxial cable in common use, 50-Ω and 75-Ω. The 50-Ω cable is used for digital transmission only, whereas the 75-Ω is used for both digital and analogue transmission. There are many differences in the characteristics of the two types of cable, one being the data rate when used for digital transmission: the 50-Ω will support speeds of up to 10 Mbit/s, whereas the 75-Ω will go up to 50 Mbit/s. The principal differences are discussed under the *baseband* and *broadband* sub-sections in the next chapter. Both have good error rates, 1 bit in 10^7 bits and 1 in 10^9 bits respectively, but care must be taken with the installation of both, as crushing the cable affects its characteristics.

3.3 FIBRE OPTIC CABLE

A *fibre optic* cable consists of a very thin, flexible, glass or plastic strand, down which light can be transmitted by reflection off the tube's internal walls, as illustrated in Fig. 3.3.

Fibre optic cable holds considerable promise for local area networks, as it can operate with much greater speeds and distances than coaxial cable. It also has the considerable advantage of having the lowest error rate, around 1 bit in error every 10^{10} bits transmitted, and of being immune to the sorts of electrical interference which can disrupt ordinary cables. This factor, along with the difficulties in tapping into a fibre cable, makes it invaluable for military and industrial uses. At present, however, only 9% of available LANs are based on fibre optic, representing around 3% of the market, although many use fibre links for traffic between LANs (Chapter 16). The major problem with fibre optic cable, apart from the high cost (which is showing signs of falling), is the proliferation of standards for the cable itself and for the light source which transmits the signal.

Fibre optic transmission requires the conversion of the electrical signals from a station into light. This is done by a *light source*, of which there are two types, the *Light-Emitting Diode* (LED) and the *Injection Laser Diode* (ILD). In addition to the two types of light source, there are two basic types of cable, *mono-mode* (or *single-mode*) and *multi-mode*. The incompatibility of these cables, and the fact that there are no connectors to enable them to be mixed in one system, has hindered the development of fibre optic in the LAN market.

Mono-mode fibre is designed to carry one wavelength of light, and is very thin, typically 8 to 9 μm in diameter. This makes it very attractive in hostile environments and crowded cable ducts. It has been used very successfully by PTTs for long distance trunk connections, as it supports greater data rates over longer distances than multi-mode cable. A bandwidth of 1 GHz over 1 km is not uncommon.

Multi-mode fibre, which consists of a wider core surrounded by another fibre sleeve with a different refractive index, can be made to carry two or three different light sources, each at different frequencies. This is termed *Wavelength Division Multiplexing* (WDM), and should be compared with the other multiplexing techniques discussed in Technical Note 5 in Chapter 4. There is a price to be paid for this ability, however, in that the bandwidth falls to around 500 Mhz over 1 km.

Both cable types can support either LED or ILD light sources. LEDs are much cheaper than the laser devices, by a factor of up to 5 times, but are much lower powered and tend to spread the beam out more quickly. They are therefore suitable for short distances, of up to a few kilometres, at data rates of up to 200 Mbit/s. ILDs transmit light at a higher frequency and are required for higher speeds (greater than 1000 Mbit/s can be achieved) and longer distances.

Multi-mode cable does not require the exacting manufacturing toler-ances of single-mode fibre, and can be used effectively with LEDs over the sort of distances relevant to LANs. It is thus the favourite of LAN manufacturers. There is no agreement, however, on a standard diameter for fibre cable, particularly for the multi-mode cable where the diameters of both the inner and outer fibres must match exactly across any joining boundaries. The sizes of multi-mode cables are quoted as '*x/y*' where '*x*' is

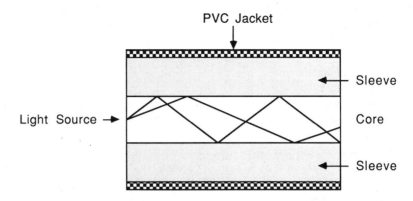

Fig. 3.3 — Construction of fibre optic cable.

the inner diameter and 'y' the outer. The uncertainty over standard sizes has certainly led to a reluctance on the part of users to commit to the installation of a system which may prove to have a limited lifetime, as even the design of the connecting plugs to join lengths of cables or to connect to stations is manufacturer-specific.

Some attempt at standardisation has been made in the USA, under the American National Standards Institute (ANSI), who have defined a 100 Mbit/s LAN called FDDI, the *Fibre Distributed Data Interface*. This uses 50/125, or 62.5/125 (as favoured by AT&T), or 85/125 multi-mode fibre. Another branch of ANSI, the Exchange Carriers Standards Association (ECSA), has however, defined a Synchronous Optical Network (SONET) which uses single mode fibre. Furthermore, IBM favour 100/140 multi-mode, while the CCITT is recommending a standard of 50/125.

Although this may seem depressing for the potential purchaser, it can be seen that, with the exception of IBM's proposed cable, most of the fibres have the same diameter (125 μm), so that joining connectors could be made to help alleviate the problem. IBM's position is particularly unfortunate as the FDDI standard uses similar protocols to IBM's token ring, and there is considerable speculation that IBM will change to 'standard' cable in the near future.

In conclusion, while fibre optic cables offer great technical potential, many of the practical details have still to be agreed. Furthermore, there are other installation disadvantages in that the coupling equipment tends to be physically very large, and the cable itself is quite delicate, requiring specialist installation. As noted, the cable is very secure, in that it is very difficult to tap; on the other hand this is a severe disadvantage when implementing some of the LAN topologies discussed in Chapter 5.

3.4   OTHER MEDIA

Wide area networking has often used various other media for cost effective communications, notably microwave, infra-red and laser. These are all point-to-point systems, usually requiring direct line of sight between the points. They have not been used to any significant degree in local area networks. Two other media do occur in LAN systems, however: ribbon cable and the electricity mains wiring.

3.4.1   Ribbon cables

Ribbon cables are simply an extension of the system commonly used to link personal computers to peripherals, particularly printers and disc drives. The cable is a flat plastic material a few inches wide, within which are buried several wires, normally in multiples of 8 plus 1. Instead of requiring the data to be transmitted serially — one 'bit' followed by the next 'bit' — a ribbon cable enables the bits to be sent in parallel. In a nine wire system the data is sent in 8 bit bytes, with the ninth wire carrying a clocking signal to synchronise the data.

Ribbon cables are cheap to manufacture, and give an end result similar to faster media — a 1 Mbit/s system, for example, effectively delivers 8 Mbit/s. Electrically it is similar to twisted pair in supporting limited speeds, but it suffers from a difficulty in tapping, and therefore is used mainly for point to point systems.

3.4.2   Mains power lines

The idea of using a building's electricity mains wiring to carry data has long been attractive in that no additional wiring is necessary, and since there is normally power in every room, equipment can be relocated very easily. The principal problem to be overcome is the prevention of data corruption from the notoriously fluctuating mains supply frequency. This is usually achieved by a system called *frequency shift keying*, a technique also used on other communications links. In this, rather than transmitting the data by changing the voltage on the medium, the frequency of the carrier signal is altered (Technical Note 6, at the end of Chapter 4).

To further reduce interference, the data is normally sent using the live and neutral wires, but returned on the earth wire. There are now several such systems on the market, offering an RS-232 interface for asynchronous data at speeds of up to 9600 bit/s. Most offer only a few channels, typically four, each of which can carry one conversation, and so they have only very limited use in a multi-user environment. They are attractive, however, in systems where a central machine polls several devices (such as remote sensors) in a controlled manner such that only one piece of data is ever transmitted at once.

Safety is, of course, an important design issue in such systems, and great care is taken to isolate the communication equipment, and the user, from the mains.

Technical Note 3: *Bandwidth and attenuation*

Strictly speaking, the *bandwidth* of a medium is the range of frequencies over which it can support transmissions. This is usually quoted in Hertz (Hz), and varies greatly with the physical properties of the medium, as noted below. Unfortunately, the term has also come into common use in data networks to mean the *data rate* which a medium can sustain, in bits per second (bit/s).

Any signal on any medium will *attenuate*, i.e. lose power or strength, over distance. The attentuation of a medium is dependent on its physical properties and on the type of transmission used. One of the major differences between copper wires and fibre optic, for example, is that the attenuation is linear with distance on fibre, but increases with the square of the distance on copper.

4

Topology and transmission

4.1   LAN TOPOLOGIES

Chapter 3 discussed transmission media. This chapter deals with two further technical aspects of LANs, namely network topology and data transmission techniques. The topology of a network is the shape of the communications link between the stations, i.e. how the stations on the network are arranged in relation to each other. There are four basic practical topologies used in LANs: star, ring, bus and tree.

4.1.1 Star networks
The simple star diagram of Fig. 4.1 illustrates the *star* topology, with each

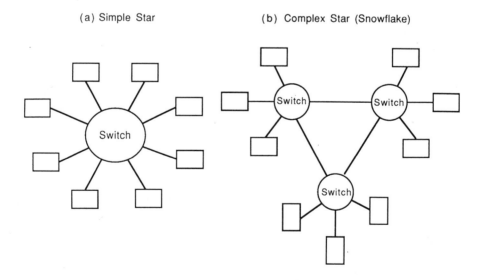

Fig. 4.1 — Star topologies

station connected to a central switch by a dedicated physical link. As noted in Chapter 2, the switch provides a path between any two devices wishing to communicate, either physically in a circuit switch or logically in a packet switch. The main advantages of a star network are that access to the network, i.e. the decision on when a station can and cannot transmit, is under central network control. Star networks tend to imply simple attachment hardware at each station, although the switches themselves can be complex and therefore expensive. Speeds are generally limited and the central switch is an obvious potential source of catastrophic failure.

Large star networks, with many switches linked in what is sometimes called a *snowflake* topology, form the basis of wide area networking, for example the US ARPA network, or the UK PSS network. Some 12% of LANs are based on star topologies, usually those designed around shared disc and printer servers.

4.1.2 Ring networks

As Fig. 4.2 illustrates, a *ring* network is one where the stations are connected

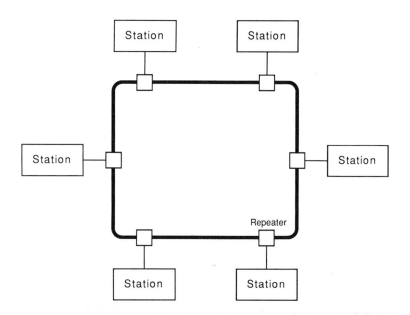

Fig. 4.2 — Ring topology.

by a loop of cable, and each connection point, called a *repeater*, is responsible for passing on each fragment of the data. The data is sent in packets, and within each station there is a controller board responsible for recognising packets sent to that station, i.e. *addressed* to that station, and for controlling access to the ring, i.e. deciding when it is clear to start transmitting. Unlike star networks, in a ring network access is not under central control, and several methods are available. These are the subject of the next chapter.

Rings have not made much impact commercially until recently, with

IBM choosing the token passing ring as their preferred LAN product. This has brought ring systems firmly back into the forefront of LAN technology. Rings can thus be expected to take a large share of the LAN market in the next few years, although they represent only some 20% of current LANs. The token ring is discussed in detail in Chapter 8.

The principal disadvantage of rings is that every station is involved in the transfer of data, and thus one failure of a repeater brings the whole network to a halt. Much effort has been devoted to solving this problem, notably by IBM for the token ring. The second disadvantage lies in the ring control mechanisms required: to start up the ring, determine that the packets are not corrupt, and prevent the same packet from going round the ring for ever because of a station fault. Some rings employ a special *monitor* station to do this job, whereas IBM have taken the approach that every station should have the capability of monitoring the ring. Rings have two major advantages: the backing of IBM, and their ability to take advantage of the very high speeds potentially offered by fibre optic cables. Proteon, for example, offer an 80 Mbit/s ring, and the 100 Mbit/s FDDI LAN described in Chapter 16 is ring based. Rings can also overcome some of the distance limitations between stations often imposed by other topologies.

4.1.3 Bus networks

Bus networks are the most common LANs, some 50% being based on this topology. They have no switches and, in their simplest form, no repeaters, but simply share a common, linear communications medium, as shown in Fig 4.3. Each station requires a *tap* (hardware for attachment to the

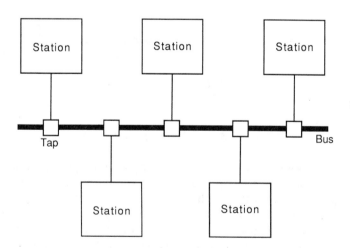

Fig. 4.3 — Bus topology.

medium), which must be capable of delivering the signal to all the stations on the bus.

The data are again sent in packets, and each station 'hears' all the transmissions, picking up those addressed to it. Most bus networks have the advantage of being passive, i.e. all of the active components are in the stations, and a failure affects only that one station. They can be somewhat limited in distance, however, and since usually only one station at a time can transmit there has to be a complex access mechanism at each station.

The most significant bus network to date is *Ethernet*, invented by Xerox in the mid 1970s (Metcalf & Boggs 1976), and now adopted as an international standard. Ethernet is examined in detail in Chapter 7. It should be noted that some LANs claim to be bus networks, but are in fact *chained* — each station is responsible for passing the message to the next, just like a ring but with no loop involved. This is similar to the *multi-drop* technique, commonly used in wide area networking (Deasington 1984).

4.1.4   Tree networks

The *tree* topology is a generalisation of the bus topology in that the cable can be made to branch down many side shoots by the use of a cable splitting device (Fig. 4.4). As in a bus, each transmission propagates down each

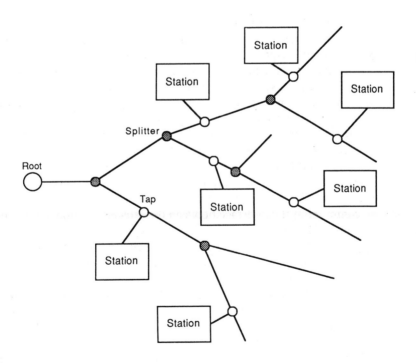

Fig. 4.4 — Tree topology.

branch of the tree to all stations. Tree topologies are significant in broadband networks, which are described below, although one of the commonest baseband LANs, ARCNET, is also described as having an 'arbitrary tree topology'.

4.2 TRANSMISSION AND DATA ENCODING

The next technical aspect of LANs to be discussed is the form of transmission of the data, i.e. how the bits themselves are sent across whatever medium has been chosen. There are two major types of transmission, termed *baseband* and *broadband*. The basic difference is that baseband transmission uses digital signalling while broadband uses analogue. This difference implies different ways of encoding the data onto the medium, and different ways of sharing (multiplexing) the medium between several transmissions.

Before examining these, it should be stressed that while in the early days of LANs there was a great 'which is better?' debate, this has largely subsided, owing to the fact that broadband LANs address specific situations, whereas baseband LANs cover almost all other LAN requirements. Only around 11% or so of LANs are broadband, with their market share, particularly outside the USA well under 10%.

4.2.1 Baseband networks

The word *baseband* strictly means that the original signal is transmitted without modulation, i.e. at its original frequency. For LANs, the word is used to mean that digital signalling is used, with the whole bandwidth of the medium being used to carry one single transmission. Since only one information channel can be handled on the medium at any one time, it is necessary to transmit data at very high speeds and to share the channel capacity, by some time division multiplexing method, between the users (see Technical Note 5 at the end of the chapter).

The result is a high speed network which is quite short (of the order of one or two kilometres) with a complex scheme for dividing the time into sections for the users. Access to most baseband networks requires some sort of computer at the interface between the attached station and the network. Because of the digital signalling, baseband networks are relatively simple to engineer, have simple topologies and are cheap enough to use for linking a moderate number of low cost stations; hence the fact that baseband networks dominate the LAN market.

The digital signals on a baseband LAN are usually represented by two voltage levels, negative for 0, and positive for 1, with the bits being transmitted serially along the medium. The main problem with this approach is that it is difficult to determine where one bit ends and the next begins, as two 'ones' together would not change the voltage. The receiver must be synchronised with the transmitter, and this is normally done using a system called *Manchester encoding*, in which the codes themselves keep the stations in synchronisation, and are thus termed *self clocking* (Technical Note 4 at the end of the chapter).

Most of the remainder of this book is concerned with the technical details of baseband networks, and with a description of some of the more popular of these. The rest of this chapter is dedicated to broadband networks.

4.2.2   Broadband networks

Broadband networks use modulated analogue signals, known as *carrier signals*, to transmit data. A medium, usually 75-Ω coaxial cable, is chosen which can support transmissions over a wide range of frequencies, generally up to 300 or 400 MHz. The total frequency of the medium is divided into a number of narrower bands (channels), by frequency division multiplexing, and each is used independently to provide a range of services. For example, one channel could run an IBM 3270 terminal service to mainframes, another could link PCs, a third could be used for word processing, and so on. In this manner, broadband networks can support many thousands of terminals and host computers, although they may appear to be on different *logical* networks from each other. A station on the network is usually allocated to one particular channel, although it may be able to select the service required on demand. This is analogous to the scheme used for ordinary radio transmissions, in which the receiver can tune into one of a large number of different frequencies within one waveband.

The major advantage of broadband networks, apart from their ability to carry multiple data services, is that channels can also be assigned for analogue data, including television, voice, facsimile and security systems. Other advantages result from the long distances which can be covered, since analogue signals are not distorted in the same way as digital signals. *Amplifiers* can be used to boost the signals over long distances, with coverage of up to 50 square km being typical.

The maximum bandwidth normally used for one television channel on a broadband system in the USA is 6 MHz. The bandwidth required for a data channel depends on the required speed of the data transmission. The faster the data rate required, the greater the bandwidth for each channel. For example, the full Ethernet 10 Mbit/s is now available using 18 Mhz of bandwidth, whereas the LocalNet product, produced by Sytek, offers 120 channels running at 128 kbit/s, each of which require 300 kHz of bandwidth. Thus a large number of channels can be fitted into the total bandwidth available.

Each channel in a broadband system is logically independent of every other channel, and they may be operated at different speeds and use different access methods. There are, however, devices called *channel bridges* which can link two identical channels. Each channel can be considered to be a separate *baseband* LAN, in which the same problems of access for stations sharing a channel must be solved. Many of the baseband solutions discussed later (Chapter 5) are used within channels on broadband systems; for example, CSMA/CD in the Ethernet system mentioned above.

Alternatively, channels can be dedicated to very fast transfers on a point-to-point basis.

The basic equipment for broadband networks is that used in the cable television industry, generally called CATV (Community Antenna TeleVision).CATV cable is easy to obtain, particularly in the USA, and fairly cheap. Most of the components, for example the connectors for attaching devices to the cable, are also standard CATV equipment, and as such are built to work unattended under adverse conditions for long periods. Because CATV systems, particularly the amplifiers, operate in one direction only — towards the television receiver — broadband networks are designed with two data paths for each station, one to transmit and one to receive.

Modems are required at each station to modulate and demodulate the digital signals onto the carrier signals for transmission over the network. The modems can operate on one particular frequency, or, more typically, on a pair of frequencies, one to transmit and one to receive. Modems can be made which can operate on several different frequencies and can be switched, locally or remotely, from one to another. These are called *frequency agile* modems; they make it possible for a station to access several different services. The need to use modems, which are considerably more complex than simple baseband coupling devices, can increase the cost of connecting a device to the network. Although a low speed modem for use at low frequencies on the telephone network can be made quite cheaply, a high speed radio frequency modem for use on a broadband network can be expensive.

Most broadband networks use a tree topology, as shown in Fig. 4.5,

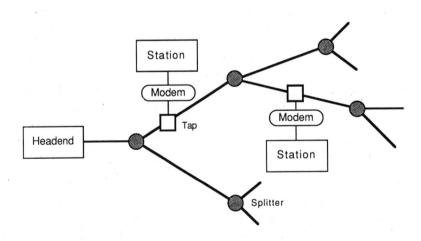

Fig. 4.5 — Typical broadband network.

using a device called a *splitter* at each branch. This sends the signals down each branch of the cable, and the data paths are provided by either one or two cables. On a dual-cable system, one cable is used by every device for transmitting information, and the other for receiving it. This will normally require two modems for each station. The cables meet at the root of the tree system, at a piece of equipment called a *headend* which receives all the transmissions from all the channels on the transmit cable, and relays them on the other cable for reception by the attached devices. The frequencies employed for the channels can be the same on the two cables, allowing the full 300–400 MHz available bandwidth to be utilised.

In the single cable system the total frequency bandwidth of the cable has to be divided between transmission and reception, and it is usual to have an approximately equal division into upper and lower halves, with an unused *guard band* between. One half is used for transmitting by every attached device, and the other for receiving. This is called a *mid-split* system, and the headend includes a *frequency translator*, which performs the function of receiving all the transmissions on the transmit channels, changing their frequencies and re-transmitting them on the appropriate receive channels. A typical allocation of channels is shown in Fig. 4.6, for a system using 5 Mbit/s channels.

	Channel	1	252-258 Mhz
	Channel	2	258-264 Mhz
Transmit	Channel	3	264-270 Mhz
	Channel	4	270-276 Mhz
	Channel	5	276-282 Mhz
	Guard Band		300 Mhz
	Channel	5	84-90 Mhz
	Channel	4	78-84 Mhz
Receive	Channel	3	72-78 Mhz
	Channel	2	66-72 Mhz
	Channel	1	60-66 Mhz

Fig. 4.6 — Typical bandwidth allocation for 5 Mbit/s channels.

To summarise, the advantages of a broadband network are the ability to mix data with voice, video and other transmissions on a common medium, the large distances covered and the large number of devices which can be supported. They are therefore ideal for campus networks and large factory complexes, but there are several disadvantages.

The first problem is the cost of the initial design and planning of the network, both in the time required and in the employment of specialist assistance. A broadband network has to be planned carefully. In order to ensure that the signal strength is equal at each tapping point, the position of every amplifier and splitter must be computed, as must the output levels at every tap. Because of this, it is very difficult, once the network is installed, to add intermediate stations on an existing branch. New branches can be added, with suitable adjustments to the amplifiers, but it is more cost effective to plan for all possible outlets at the outset. This increases the start-up costs of the network, which can be a significant part of the total network cost.

The physical location of the equipment may be a problem, particularly the amplifiers, which are not particularly small and to which access will be required. Like the modems, the amplifiers are powered from the central conductor of the cable, with a 30 V a.c. supply from the headend. The headend equipment is an obvious single point of failure, and so should be duplicated to improve reliability. All analogue devices need periodic testing and adjustment to remain within the operational specification, and for a large network this may require the permanent hiring of the necessary engineering support staff.

The final problem for the network maintainer is the general lack of standards for the CATV equipment, and for the allocation of frequencies for services. The network manager must be responsible for frequency allocation, and must ensure that new equipment from a different manufacturer will not produce noise on existing channels. An interesting report on a large broadband installation, at Brown University in the USA, which highlights many of these problems, can be found in Shipp & Webber (1982).

In conclusion, the installation of a broadband network, unlike most baseband networks, must be considered as a major corporate investment, which will only be cost effective where there is a combination of large distances, large numbers of devices, and the requirement for video or voice in addition to data. Broadband networks can also be effective, however, for hybrid LANs, where several baseband technologies may be mixed by being attached to a large capacity *backbone* broadband network.

Technical note 4: Manchester encoding
Manchester encoding achieves its clocking by always changing from a high to a low voltage, or low to high, in the middle of a bit. This is shown in the top part of Fig. 4.7, where a low-to-high change indicates a 0 bit, and a high-to-low change a 1 bit.

Because the voltage always changes, the receiver can keep in step with the transmitter. There is also a variant called *differential Manchester*, shown in the lower part of Fig. 4.7, where a 0 is signalled by the presence of a transition right at the start of the bit period, and a 1 by the absence of such a transition.

Technical note 5: Multiplexing
Multiplexing is the method whereby a medium can be shared between many users, by carrying, or appearing to carry, more than one transmission at a time. There are two main types:

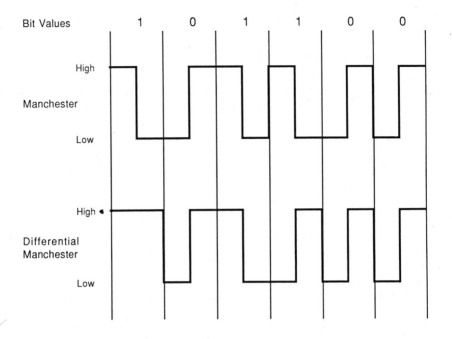

Fig. 4.7 — Examples of Manchester encoding.

Time Division Multiplexing (TDM) relies on the very high data rates achievable on some media, particularly fibre optic cables. The transmission is divided up into time slots and several slower rate data signals are interleaved to form the fast frames (Fig. 4.8). For example, there is a 2 Mbit/s

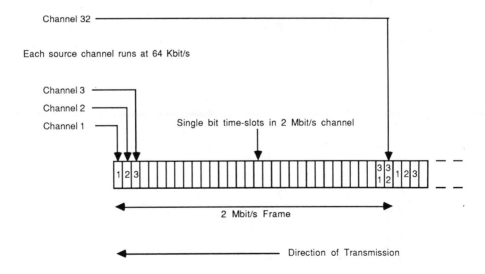

Fig. 4.8 — Example of time division multiplexing.

trunk standard for inter-PABX working which can be split up into thirty-two 64 kbit/s channels. Single bits from each of the 32 channels comprise one *frame* in the 2 Mbit/s trunk. This type of TDM is called synchronous because each time frame is fixed.

More common in LANs, however, is a form of asynchronous time division multiplexing, in which each station is given a 'turn' in which to transmit a packet. The packets are each enveloped within a frame consisting of a preamble to allow the receiver to synchronise with the transmitter, followed by the data, followed by some end-of-frame delimiter. Some examples are shown in Chapters 7, 8 and 9, and the various methods of sharing a single channel LAN are the subject of Chapter 5.

Frequency Division Multiplexing (FDM) uses the fact that most media have a high bandwidth. Since the bandwidth is typically much greater than that required for one transmission, multiple signals can be carried by sending the data on different carrier frequencies (called *channels*), well separated from each other (Fig. 4.9).

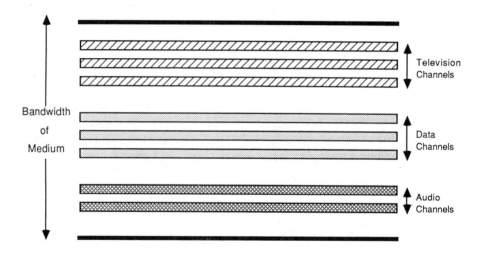

Fig. 4.9 — Example of frequency division multiplexing.

A typical example is cable television, where many TV channels are carried on one cable. Each television channel will require around 6 MHz, but the cable has a bandwidth of 300 MHz. This is the technique used by broadband local area networks.

Waveband division multiplexing (Chapter 3) is identical, but for light based systems it is usual to refer to wavelength rather than frequency.

Technical note 6: Analogue data encoding
In a broadband system which uses analogue signals, the data are encoded onto the carrier signal by one of three different techniques.

In *Amplitude Shift Keying* (ASK), the two binary values are represented by different values of the carrier signal amplitude or strength, but this system is very poor and will only work at low speeds.

In *Frequency Shift Keying* (FSK), the two values are represented by slight differences in the frequency of the carrier signal. This system works well at high frequencies.

Finally, *Phase Shift Keying* (PSK) uses changes in the phase of the carrier frequency to represent 1s and 0s.

5

LAN access control methods

The *access control* method of a LAN is the means whereby the flow of data to and from stations is controlled. Although it is often related to the topology of the LAN, some techniques can be imposed on different topologies.

5.1 POLLING

The technique of *polling* is widespread in traditional wide area networks, IBM's 3270 terminal networks for example. It relies on a *master-slave* relationship between a central server and the other stations on the LAN. Although developed for star topologies, it is commonly used in small to medium scale PC LANs, using star, bus or ring topologies.

The central server, usually a file store, simply maintains a list of the stations assigned to share its disc space, and asks each one in turn if it has any transmission to make. If it has, that station is permitted to send one or more packets to the central station. The station must then wait until it is polled again before it can send any more. It is also normal to permit data to be transferred from the master to the slave during the same transaction. Thus a dialogue such as the one in Fig. 5.1 takes place.

The obvious disadvantage of this technique is that the medium can be occupied for lengthy periods with polls to stations which have nothing to send, possibly holding up stations which are busy. It also means that any station to station transfers must be passed through the central server, and not all LAN systems will permit this. The technique depends crucially on the reliability of the central server, as any lost or corrupt polls can only be repaired centrally.

On the other hand, the system is very simple to implement, requiring no complex hardware or software in the stations. There is no problem over more than one station simultaneously trying to use the medium, and it is possible to implement different levels of priority, by polling the more

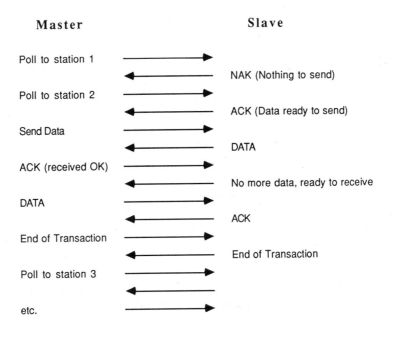

Master   Slave

Poll to station 1

NAK (Nothing to send)

Poll to station 2

ACK (Data ready to send)

Send Data

DATA

ACK (received OK)

No more data, ready to receive

DATA

ACK

End of Transaction

End of Transaction

Poll to station 3

etc.

Fig. 5.1 — Example of polling technique.

important stations more often. It is therefore commonly used for small scale networks where the rate of transactions is expected to be low.

5.2   CARRIER SENSE MULTIPLE ACCESS

Carrier Sense Multiple Access (CSMA) techniques are by far the commonest used in LANs, accounting for about 60% of those LANs which have a non-proprietary access system. The method is restricted to bus and tree LANs, the common feature being the *multiple access*: all the stations share the same physical medium, or the same channel in a broadband system.

As all the stations have equal priority, there being no polling from a central station, a station must listen to the medium to detect if it is idle or not before starting its own transmission. The listening is for another station's transmissions, the *carrier sensing* of the title. In a baseband LAN, this is normally the detection of any Manchester style transitions on the cable, there being no carrier as such. A broadband channel requires the detection of modulation of the carrier signal. CSMA LANs are also referred to as *listen before talk* LANs, for obvious reasons.

The problem with this method is that two stations could decide to transmit simultaneously, both having detected an idle medium. Furthermore it takes some time for a signal from one station to reach all the other stations on the LAN, and so there is a time after one station starts to transmit before all the other stations have detected the transmission, and therefore will not themselves try to transmit. It is possible to implement a network whereby a station simply transmits and detects a problem by the lack of an acknowledgment from the receiver if the packet is corrupted en route. This is not very efficient, however, and there are now two commonly used solutions to these problems: CSMA with *Collision Detection* (CSMA/CD), and CSMA with *Collision Avoidance* (CSMA/CA).

5.2.1   CSMA/CD

CSMA/CD was originally developed, by the Xerox Corporation, as *Ethernet,* and the original version is fully described in Metcalf & Boggs (1976). As explained above, before a packet can be transmitted the network must be clear of traffic, and so the transmitter first listens to the network (carrier sensing). When the LAN is idle the station transmits its own packet but at the same time keeps monitoring—'listening' to the network. It is possible that two or more devices decide to transmit at about the same time, and when this happens the voltage level (on a baseband LAN) will be too low. This is called a *collision,* and when a transmitting station detects it, it stops transmitting the packet and sends out a very high *jamming signal,* to ensure that the collision will be detected by other transmitting stations.

The transmitting stations involved in the collision will each stop trying to transmit for random time intervals, before trying again. This is termed *backing off.* If another collision is detected, the station will double its mean random delay time and back off again. This is known as *binary exponential backoff,* and a station will attempt to transmit for up to 16 times before reporting an error condition. It will be appreciated that collisions are much more likely when there is a heavy demand on the network, but in practice the method works well for devices with intermittent requirements to transmit.

The main practical problem with CSMA/CD networks is the need to ensure that collisions are guaranteed to be detected. Consider the worst case situation of two stations on a baseband bus, as far apart as possible (Fig. 5.2).

If station A transmits first, its packet must be large enough for the start of it to reach station B and, assuming station B starts to transmit just before station A's packet reaches it, for station B's jamming signal (it will detect the collision first) to reach station A, *while station A is still transmitting,* so that station A can also detect the collision. This means that a maximum end-to-end transmission time and a minimum packet size must be imposed. The minimum packet size is the number of bits required to transmit for a time of about twice the propagation delay of the LAN. It thus varies with the speed of the LAN.

All CSMA/CD LANs are a compromise between covering a reasonable area at a reasonable speed, without carrying too much overhead in each packet. In the Ethernet version, which runs at 10 Mbit/s, the minimum packet size is fixed at 64 bytes, the maximum end-to-end transmission time is 44.95 microseconds and the overall distance on coaxial cable is 1.5 km. The problem is more acute on broadband LANs, where the worst case involves

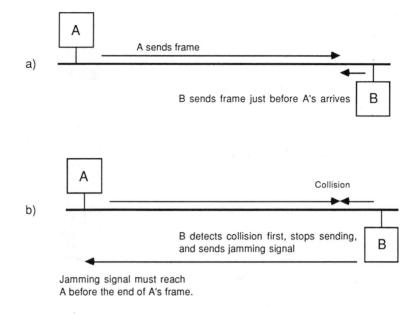

Fig. 5.2 — Worst case collision example.

two stations near to each other but as far as possible from the headend: the signal has to travel up to the headend then down almost to the second station, and then the jamming signal has to come back again, making four times the propagation delay. As broadband networks can be very long, CSMA/CD channels tend to be run at low speeds, for otherwise the packet size would be unacceptably large. There are other problems with broadband CSMA/CD, notably that collisions can only really be detected by a station comparing its transmissions with what it itself sees on the receive channel. Given the number of amplifiers and splitters the signal is passing through this is not always reliable. To solve this problem, CSMA/CA is frequently used.

5.2.2 CSMA/CA
Carrier sense multiple access with collision avoidance attempts to detect a collision before any actual data is transmitted, rather than trying to recover from a lost data packet. The technique is explained at length by Colvine (1983), but briefly the essential difference between collision avoidance and collision detection is that a station tries to claim the LAN by transmitting a short frame, called a *carrier burst,* which on a broadband LAN is over a wide range of frequencies. Adjacent stations could detect a collision in this initial burst, at which point they would back-off as normal. Any station seeing a carrier burst will not try to transmit until the end of the subsequent data packet has been seen.

The transmitting station then listens again to the LAN (Fig. 5.3) to detect any carrier bursts coming from remote stations. When it is sure that every

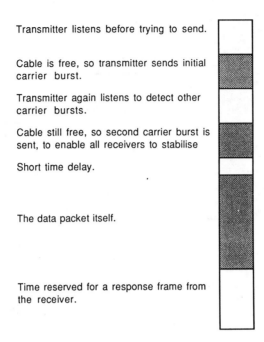

Transmitter listens before trying to send.

Cable is free, so transmitter sends initial carrier burst.

Transmitter again listens to detect other carrier bursts.

Cable still free, so second carrier burst is sent, to enable all receivers to stabilise

Short time delay.

The data packet itself.

Time reserved for a response frame from the receiver.

Fig. 5.3 — Illustration of CSMA/CA.

station has seen the carrier burst it can transmit the data, sometimes with additional gaps to allow for address recognition and the adjustment of automatic gain controls in the receiver (to ensure that the receiver can pick up the signal of the following packet, given the strength of the initial part). Note that, even if the first station's carrier burst is swamped by a similar burst from a remote station, by the time it reaches that remote station, the carrier burst going in the opposite direction will have been seen by the first station, which will be in its listening gap. It will therefore back off and let the second station transmit. This technique allows very short packets to be used, and is very popular on broadband and slower baseband LANs.

5.3   TOKEN PASSING

Token passing can be thought of as a form of distributed polling, where instead of one central authority sending out polls, a single poll or *token* permanently circulates around the stations in some sequence. It is applicable to both ring and bus topologies, but, as it is logically a circulatory system, is perhaps easier to understand when applied to a ring network.

5.3.1   Token ring access

The token is a small, unique, immediately recognisable frame. On an idle ring, i.e. when no stations wish to transmit (Fig. 5.4(a)), the token simply rotates round the ring, being passed from one station to the next. When a

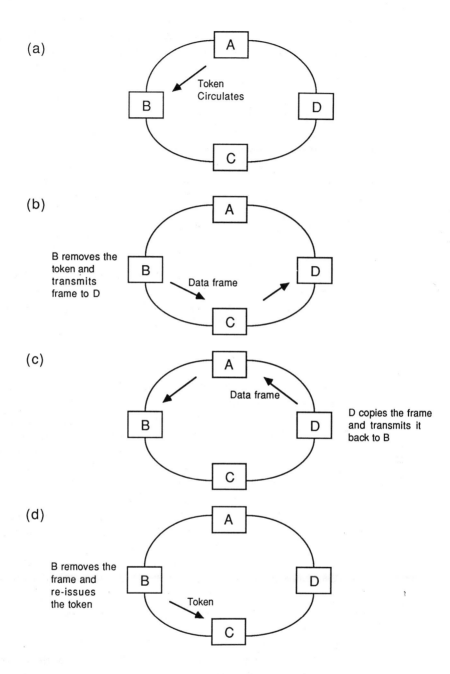

Fig. 5.4 — Token-passing ring operation.

station receives the token, it has the opportunity to transmit any data packet which it has waiting. It does this by changing the token packet into the start of a data packet and then appending its data (Fig. 5.4(b)). The data packet is

passed round the ring to the receiver, who copies it bit by bit into an internal
buffer, then passes it to the next station round the ring (Fig 5.4(c)). It will
eventually return to the sender, who will remove it from the ring. When the
transmission is finished, the sending station must regenerate the token frame
and pass it onto the next station (Figure 5.4(d)).

This is the technique used in the IBM and IEEE 802.5 token rings,
discussed in Chapter 8. There are other types but they operate essentially on
the same principle. The token passing method is less efficient than CSMA
when the LAN is idle, because a station must wait for the token to arrive, but
under heavy load it guarantees a fair share of the LAN for all the stations,
because a station must pass the token on once its data packet has passed
round the ring. The token scheme can also be used to provide unequal access
to stations, as Chapter 8 will demonstrate.

The major problem with token passing schemes is in dealing with the loss
or corruption of the token. For example, a machine may crash just when it
has taken the token in order to transmit. It is also possible to reach the faulty
state of having two tokens on the ring, which may lead to a collision. Many
rings have monitor stations to detect and correct such error conditions, and
these can also cope with starting up the ring. The IEEE ring tackles these
problems by building ring monitoring functions into *every* station.

5.3.2   Token bus

Token passing on a bus is similar in operation to that on a ring with the
difference that the sequential flow of control from station to station is not
automatic. As all the stations on the bus can physically pick up every
transmission, they have to be organised into a logical 'ring' sequence. This is
done by each device having the responsibility for periodically searching for
new stations attached to the bus which wish to join the 'ring'. At predeter-
mined intervals, each station, while it has control of the token, will send out
a special poll which only those stations not in the 'ring' can respond to. If a
response arrives, the sending station will modify the address it currently
knows to be the next station, and will tell the station which used to be next in
the sequence that a new station has just joined.

There usually has to be some form of contention resolution when more
than one station wishes to join the 'ring'. This is discussed further in Chapter
9. A station wishing to remove itself from the 'ring' waits until it has the
token, then informs the sequentially adjacent stations that they are now
neighbours in the 'ring'.

Apart from the complexity of attaching new stations to the logical ring,
the scheme enjoys the same advantages and disadvantages as the token ring.
In addition, however, it is possible to implement more flexible priority
schemes than on a physical ring. For example, a device can be included in the
sequence more than once, so that devices which often need to use the
network have a larger share of the capacity. Further, some devices may
never need to transmit but wish only to listen to the network and receive
data. These need not be included in the logical sequence of control, but they

can still hear every transmission. Unlike many other techniques, the token bus can be used for applications in which it is vital that access be obtained to the network within a guaranteed time interval, for example in process control and monitoring.

It is for this reason that token bus is the basis for the MAP protocols which are used for automated manufacturing applications. The system used, IEEE 802.4, is discussed in Chapter 9, and MAP itself in Chapter 16.

5.4   SLOTTED RING

Many other techniques have been suggested and tried for ring networks but the principal one, at least in the UK, is the *empty slot*. The empty slot technique can be thought of as a variant of the token passing method because it is the receipt of an empty packet which implies permission to use the network.

The empty slot technique was largely developed as a working system in the Computer Laboratory of the University of Cambridge; hence it is most commonly called the *Cambridge ring*, although strictly this title applies only to a specific implementation of the empty slot technique. It is described by Cole (1982) but the following is a brief summary. A station cannot transmit until an empty packet, which is always circulating, arrives (Fig. 5.5). On receipt of the fixed length empty packet, or slot, the transmitting station inserts its own address and data, and the destination address, and passes the packet on round the ring. The destination station recognises its address, reads the data, and marks a field in the packet as read, before passing the packet on round the ring.

The packet then travels back round to the transmitting station, which marks the packet as empty again and must then pass it on round the ring; the station is not permitted to use the packet again on that turn. Note that the packet is very small, with only 16 bits available for data, out of a total of 40 bits in the frame, and so larger transmissions must be split up by the stations into 16-bit chunks. This is the major technical disadvantage of the Cambridge ring compared to the token ring, as a token ring station can transmit a complete long frame whenever it has the token.

The empty slot ring is easy to implement and is capable of very high transmission speeds. A new fast ring has been developed which operates at 60 Mbit/s, although to date implementations in the field run at only 10 Mbit/s. It is inherently stable and fair to all users because each station can only use the slot once before passing it on empty. In practice, the small slot and high speed combine to allow user data to be transmitted at 1 Mbit/s or more between devices attached to a 10 Mbit/s ring.

As the load on the ring increases so the time between receiving empty slots increases, thus regulating the traffic on the ring. Despite some popularity within UK academic circles, the Cambridge ring has never achieved a large market. This is partly due to the relatively high cost of connecting a station (as chip sets for the purpose have only recently become available), but mostly it is due to the lack of support from the international standards

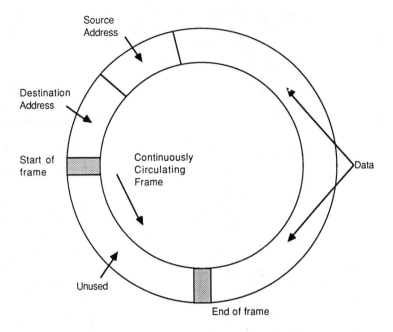

Fig. 5.5 — Example of a slotted ring.

bodies. There is, however, some European-backed effort on standardisation.

Part 3
LAN architectures

The purpose of this part is to present in some detail what are perceived to be the most important LANs, in that they either have a large market share already, or are under study by the relevant standards authorities. The relationships between the various standardisation bodies and the work they have done, particularly in the area of networking software, is the subject of Part 4.

It is clear, however, that any LAN which forms the basis of such standards is going to have a bright long-term future — hence the discussion of CSMA/CD, token ring and token bus networks, as defined by the International Standards Organisation, in subsequent chapters. This part begins, however, with a chapter on some of the non-standard networks, which are not *open* systems but are instead aimed at satisfying the existing PC market.

6

Personal computer networks

With over 100 products to choose from, it is obviously a difficult task to select a representative few to illustrate the range of systems and facilities on offer. The following five networks are either in some way typical of their kind, such as INFAPLUG, HINET, and LAN/PC, or are strong market leaders, such as ARCNET and PC-Network. The chapter concentrates on the physical aspects of the networks, the important subject of software being deferred to the next part. A major difficulty in choosing representative LANs to describe is that these products are constantly being upgraded and redesigned, so that some of the details described may not apply to what is in the field at the time of reading. It should be understood that these particular networks were chosen merely to illustrate — their inclusion does not constitute any endorsement of the system or of its manufacturer.

6.1 INFAPLUG

The *INFAPLUG* network, from *INFA Communications*, is typical of the low cost wiring replacement LAN, aimed at linking stations using their RS-232 ports.

The topology of the LAN is a ring, using 75-Ω coaxial cable or twisted pair. Instead of linking directly to the stations, the cable links *sockets*, which can be wall mounted rather like power sockets. The stations attach to the ring via a cable from their RS-232 port (Fig. 6.1). At the end of the cable is a plug which contains the necessary repeater electronics and a microprocessor to control access to the LAN. The sockets are relatively simple devices, which reduces the likelihood of ring failures, and are also fairly cheap. Thus sockets can be placed wherever there may be a need for an outlet, but the relatively expensive plug need only be bought for each actual station.

The plugs are powered from a central power supply which is carried round the ring. There is no central monitor station, however, and the software in each plug performs simple error correction. The speed of the interface is limited to 9600 bit/s per station, and the raw speed of the ring is 115 Kbit/s, and so although the LAN in theory can support up to 255 stations, only a relatively small number of simultaneous transmissions can be supported in practice. For many applications, however, this is unlikely to present a problem.

The access method of the LAN is somewhat different from those examined in the previous chapter. The ring works by transmitting small

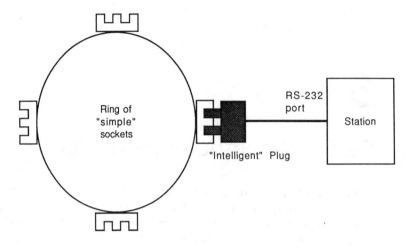

Fig. 6.1 — Schematic of INFAPLUG system.

packets, up to 64 bytes long, and each station is capable of *buffering* (storing) an entire packet in the memory in its plug. When a station wishes to transmit, the plug first waits for any passing packet to finish. It can then start to transmit its own packet, any new incoming packet being held in a buffer in the plug. When the station has finished transmitting its own packet, it must transmit any that are buffered in the plug. The station can be said to be inserting its packet into the ring traffic and thus this type of access is termed *packet insertion*. It is a development of an earlier system called – *register insertion* in which single bytes could be buffered.

Unlike the token ring method, this method implies that each arc of the ring can be carrying a different packet. The system is therefore efficient for slow rings with small packet sizes. A plug also buffers the data intended for its own station, and the data can be presented to the station using one of the standard flow control procedures, such as XON/XOFF. The buffering of data also means that error checking and recovery software is in the plug and not in the end station. It also means that the transmitting station can operate at a different speed from the receiver.

There are two ways of establishing a connection between two plugs: under program control from a PC attached to a plug, or from a third party teletype station, which can set up a connection between two other plugs. The latter method can be used to enable PCs to be connected to shared peripherals, printers for example, without any modification to the software on the PC. Apart from a simple file transfer program, available for IBM-PCs, there is no requirement for any intelligence in the stations, and thus INFAPLUG is a good example of the wiring replacement LAN.

6.2   HINET

Apricot Computer's HINET is a typical example of a shared filestore network, aimed at supporting a range of PCs from different manufacturers, particularly IBM and Apricot. Attachment to the LAN is via interface boards which slot onto the computer's internal bus, rather than by use of the RS-232 ports.

The heart of the system is the *network controller*, which comprises a hard disc storage unit with a capacity of up to 184 Mbytes, a tape streamer and a system printer; these can be shared over the LAN by up to 63 stations. The LAN is a bus topology (Fig. 6.2) and the raw data rate is 500 Kbit/s. The

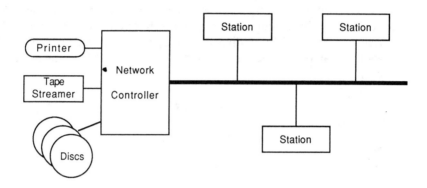

Fig. 6.2 — Schematic of HINET system.

controller treats all the stations as *slaves* and uses a polling technique to control access. The medium can either be a ribbon cable or twisted pairs.

HINET is aimed at the office automation market, and like other similarly targeted LANs offers many features particularly attractive to that market. For example, data integrity is obviously important, and HINET has an optional duplicate disc system which copies every disc access to the main controller. This gives an instant backup in the event of failure.

Another important feature, discussed further in Chapter 14, is access to corporate wide area networks. This is achieved through *gateway stations* which support, for example, IBM 3270 protocols. Links to the telex network and dial-up access to remote computers are also offered.

Finally, Apricot Computers, in common with many other LAN manufacturers, make a range of workstations which have the necessary attachment hardware and software built-in. In the case of HINET products, they range from IBM-PC compatibles to advanced graphics stations.

6.3   PERSONAL COMPUTER NETWORK

IBM's Personal Computer Network (PC-Network) has been included largely because of its share of the market. Its main influence on LAN development has been in the establishment of a large user base of IBM-PCs connecting to the network via the NETBIOS software interface, which is examined in Chapter 13. Although regarded by some to be an interim solution while IBM developed the token ring, PC-Network is interesting as a rare example of a small scale broadband network. Unlike HINET, its design aim is to permit any PC with a suitable hard disc to be a file server for other PCs on the LAN, i.e. there is no single central controller, but a series of smaller logical clusters of PCs all sharing one LAN.

Like most broadband LANs, PC-Network has a tree topology, in this case with a simplified headend, called a *fixed frequency translator unit*. There is only one data channel in operation, but other services such as voice and video can be added, as on other broadband LANs. The PCs attach to devices called *splitters*, each of which can support up to eight PCs. A network can be as simple as a single translator unit and one splitter, but can also be extended by adding a *base expander* to which eight additional splitters can be attached, giving a maximum of 72 PCs on the network (Fig. 6.3).

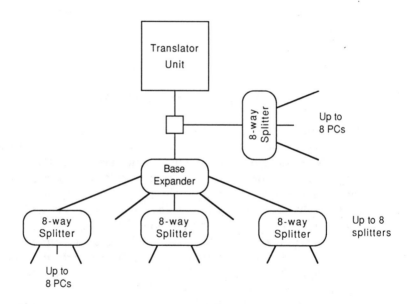

Fig. 6.3 — Schematic of PC-Network.

The base expander provides the only amplification needed in the system, as it is able to drive PCs up to 300 m from the headend. The network can be expanded with suitable amplification and cabling to encompass 255 stations, and by upgrading the headend a full scale broadband network of up to 1000 stations can be achieved.

The PC-Network runs at 2 Mbit/s and uses the CSMA/CD access method. The really important aspect of this LAN is its software, both in the network interface and in IBM's PC-Network program, which has been supported on many other LANs. The software is still aimed at the shared filestore approach, and there is no direct method of station to station transfer. IBM also produce a baseband system with the same name, which provides similar facilities but with simpler technology.

6.4   ARCNET

ARCNET (Attached Resource Computer NETwork), is manufactured by the *Datapoint Corporation*, and was the world's first commercial LAN, having been installed from 1977. Datapoint now claim to have installed over 9000 worldwide, which establishes ARCNET as having one of the largest user bases. In its early years ARCNET was used to link Datapoint's own office workstations, its main design aim being to relieve those stations of networking processing overheads; it was thus a proprietary, closed network. Recently, however, many other machines (particularly micros running various different operating systems) have been added, thus increasing the suitability of ARCNET as a general purpose LAN. In addition, several other manufacturers have used ARCNET as the basis of their own LAN products.

The ARCNET topology is very unusual, being described as an *arbitrary tree*. As Fig. 6.4 shows, each station connects to a hub, which is a signal repeater and may be active or passive. An active hub re-generates the signal and can have up to eight stations, or other hubs, attached to it. A passive hub provides a non-regenerative link between the station and the LAN cable and can have up to four ports on it. A station can be up to 30 m from a passive hub or 600 m from an active hub, with inter-hub distances similar. The hubs can be connected in any manner, except that two passive hubs cannot be connected directly. At least one company offers a hub-to-hub fibre optic link which increases the distance to 1.2 km.

A total of 255 stations can be attached, and a token passing scheme running at 2.5 Mbit/s is used for media access; it is not compatible, however, with the IEEE token ring system described in Chapter 8. The network interface boards are designed to handle all the low level access protocols and are capable of storing up to four full size packets (512 bytes each). One of the main difficulties in attaching slow stations to fast LANs is that, while the LAN may be reliable, the stations may not be able to keep up, and this results in lost packets and many re-transmissions. The ARCNET access protocol attempts to overcome this difficulty. When a station wishes to transmit, it first sends a small request packet to the receiver asking if it has enough room to store another packet. Only if the sender gets a positive reply will it try to send the packet. The station will then wait for a 'positive receipt of packet' message from the receiver before creating a token for the next station.

The protocol itself is loosely based on the wide area technique of *byte synchronous* (BYSYNC) transfers, i.e. whole bytes are sent to indicate start-of-message, end-of-message, positive and negative acknowledge, etc. This should be compared with the acknowledgment procedures on the token ring described in Chapter 8.

Datapoint Corporation manufacture a wide range of office products

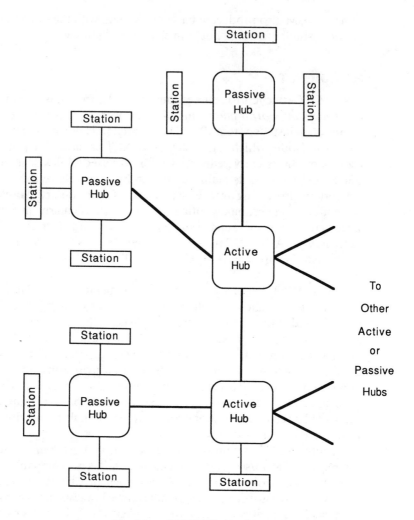

Fig. 6.4 — ARCNET hub architecture.

which exploit ARCNET, and offer a link to their Information Switching Exchange, which can handle voice, data and text messages. Various companies produce IBM-PC boards for ARCNET, as well as for the Apple, Sirius and Apricot machines.

6.5   LAN/PC

The final example of a PC network is a full scale broadband network, manufactured by *Interactive Systems/3M. LAN/PC* is designed solely for the IBM-PC and compatibles, a PC card providing the media access control and connecting the PC directly to the 75-Ω coaxial cable.

LAN/PC offers five 2.5 Mbit/s channels, each occupying 6 MHz of bandwidth, and on each channel up to 255 PCs can be handled. One interesting feature of LAN/PC is that the Novell Netware operating system is used. This is described in detail in Chapter 13, but briefly it is a network operating system which runs in conjunction with PC-DOS or MS-DOS. It permits a wide range of file and peripheral sharing and has been implemented on most of the common baseband LANs.

Its use on LAN/PC means that it is possible to connect many baseband LANs using the broadband LAN as a carrier. As the broadband LAN can have a radius of up to 14 miles, this can be very advantageous. As far as the PCs are concerned, they are all on the one logical LAN, linked by the common software. The bridges between the LANs are constructed using PCs themselves. In addition to the processor card, and the LAN/PC card, a card to access the desired baseband LAN is added together with another card which performs the matching between the two LANs. This card is obviously specific to the baseband LAN, and may have to do considerable speed matching and buffering.

7

IEEE 802.3 CSMA/CD (Ethernet)

7.1 HISTORICAL BACKGROUND

Ethernet, which was originally developed and patented in 1975, began as a research project to link personal workstations at the Xerox Palo Alto Research Centre. Its CSMA/CD technique is explained in detail in Metcalf & Boggs (1976). In 1980 Digital Equipment Corporation, Intel, and Xerox adopted a joint development policy, and published a revised specification for a faster (10 Mbit/s) CSMA/CD bus, under the trademark 'Ethernet', referred to as Ethernet 1.0. The Institute of Electrical and Electronic Engineers (IEEE) Project 802, the structure of which is outlined in Chapter 10, took Ethernet as the starting point for its CSMA/CD LAN standard, and Ethernet 2.0 was introduced in 1982 to come more into line with the IEEE's project 802.3 proposals. Unfortunately, Ethernet 2.0 and IEEE 802.3 are not identical, although they are able to co-exist on the same cable. As time passes it is likely that all manufacturers will produce products conforming to the IEEE specification, which is now an International Standard (ISO DIS 8802/3), and so incompatibility will cease to be a problem.

Since the first IEEE specification was announced for a 10 Mbit/s CSMA/CD network over coaxial cable, IEEE have continued to develop other CSMA/CD variations, notably CSMA/CD on broadband, over 'thin' coaxial cable and over twisted pair. The first part of this chapter describes the original IEEE 802.3 specification, and the later sections the variations.

7.2 METHOD OF OPERATION

The Carrier Sense Multiple Access with Collision Detection (CSMA/CD) media access method has already been described in Chapter 5. To recap briefly, all the stations on the LAN share a common bus transmission medium. To transmit, a station waits for a quiet period (a period when no-one else is transmitting), and then sends the message in bit serial form, i.e. one bit following another serially along the cable. If the message *collides* with that of another station then each transmitting station will detect the collision and will send a few extra *jamming* bytes to ensure that all stations also see it. The two stations will then remain silent for random intervals (*backoff*), before trying to transmit again.

To ensure that a collision will be detected, each packet must be large enough to occupy the whole length of the bus. The packet size is a function of the speed of transmission: basically the higher the speed the larger the minimum packet, or the shorter the bus. The IEEE specification attempts to compromise to give a reasonable bus length at a reasonable speed without too large a packet size.

7.3   MEDIUM ACCESS CONTROL FRAME FORMATS

The *medium access control (MAC) frame* is the envelope within which the station's data message is sent: its format is shown in Fig. 7.1.

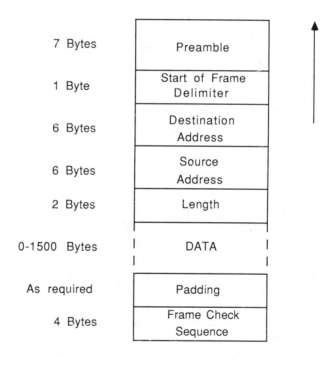

Fig. 7.1 — Format of IEEE 802.3 CSMA/CD frame.

The frame is transmitted from top to bottom, and within each byte from left to right (least to most significant bit). The elements are as follows:

Preamble field   This field is a seven byte sequence of alternating 'one' and 'zero' bit values. The system uses Manchester encoding (see Chapter 4) and this field enables each receiver to reach a steady state synchronisation with the transmitter.

Start frame delimiter field   This is a one byte field with the bit sequence '10101011'. It indicates the start of the frame.

Address fields   Each frame contains the address of the intended recipient (the *destination address*), and of the transmitting station (the *source address*). Although the specification allows for either 2 byte or 6 byte addresses, the normal practice is to use 6 bytes (48 bits). These addresses are normally allocated centrally, by IEEE, with manufacturers being allocated blocks of addresses. Thus all equipment from one manufacturer will normally have the same top few bytes of address.

The first two bits of the address have special significance. The first bit of the destination address indicates whether this is the address of an individual station ('0') or a group of stations ('1'). This enables one message to be sent to a group of stations with only one transmission, since all the stations on the LAN receive every packet. Such addresses are termed *multicast* addresses. The second bit indicates whether the address is globally ('0') or locally ('1') administered. This avoids any possible duplication of addresses between IEEE-specified stations and any 'home grown' stations.

There is one special multicast address, called the *broadcast* address, which has the value 'all ones'. This is a message intended for all stations.

Length field   This is the value of the number of bytes in the data field of the packet. It is in the interpretation of this field that the IEEE specification differs from the Ethernet 2.0 specification. Ethernet uses this field as an indicator of the type of higher level protocol carried in the data field, and the length of the data is found within the data field. The values used for this field in Ethernet are, however, defined to be greater than any valid length for an IEEE frame, the maximum frame length being 1518 bytes. It is therefore possible for a station to operate to both standards simultaneously, as it can distinguish the standard in use within each frame from the value of this field.

Data and pad fields   The data field can contain any number of bytes of any value, up to the maximum frame limit of 1518 bytes. If the number of data bytes is such that the minimum packet size required for CSMA/CD will not be met, then the required number of extra bytes is added to the end of the data field, in the pad field. For the 10 Mbit/s LAN the minimum frame size is 64 bytes, but this will vary for the other versions of CSMA/CD.

Frame check sequence field   This is a cyclic redundancy check, designed to detect bit errors within the frame. It covers all of the bytes, starting at the destination address, and is four bytes long. Any error in the FCS will cause the frame to be ignored, as will a frame which is too short or too long.

7.4   PHYSICAL COMPONENTS

Physically, a typical connection of a station to the cable is shown in Fig. 7.2. It comprises the transmission medium, a Medium Attachment Unit (MAU), an Attachment Unit Interface cable and a controller board within the station.

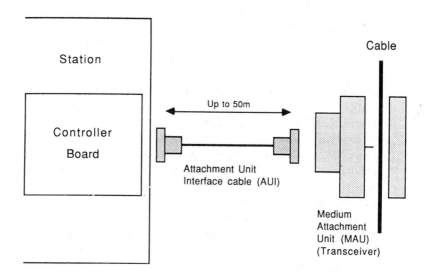

Fig. 7.2 — Typical CSMA/CD station connection.

The cable itself is a very stiff form of 50-Ω coaxial cable, the material of the outer jacket depending on the degree of physical protection required. The normal cable for use within a building has a PVC jacket, which is coloured yellow for ease of identification. The cable is marked at 2.5 m intervals with dark rings to indicate the optimum points for placing a MAU, more commonly known as a *transceiver*. Transceivers should only be placed on the cable at the marked points in order to reduce the signal reflections inevitably introduced by each transceiver.

The transceiver performs the task of transmitting the frames onto the cable and receiving them from it. It also monitors the signal levels on the medium, acts as an electrical isolator between the station and the medium, and detects collisions and other error conditions; these it signals to the controller board in the station. There are two types of transceiver. The first can be clamped onto the cable, a pin making contact with the central coaxial conductor, and is known as a *bee-sting* or *vampire*. The second, which makes a 'butt-join' connection using *barrel connectors*, requires the cable to be cut. The fact that a bee-sting type of tap can be added or removed to the cable without disrupting the network is an advantage, although in practice it can be difficult to make a good contact with the inner conductor of the cable.

The transceiver communicates with, and is powered from, the station via an *Attachment Unit Interface* (AUI) cable, which is normally coloured blue and attaches to the controller board in the station. As the signals which are passed along this cable (commonly called the transceiver cable or *drop* cable) as well as the connectors are part of the specification, it is possible to connect one manufacturer's transceivers to another's station. There are, however, some optional testing signals defined, which some transceivers may not support. The arrangement of having the transceiver remote from the station — the drop cable can be up to 50 m long — means that the main cable can be installed securely in ducts or under floors. Furthermore, as transceivers are relatively inexpensive, it is possible to achieve some flexibility in the location of equipment by installing more transceivers than are immediately needed. The controller, which is specific to the type of station, implements all the other CSMA/CD functions; e.g. the random back-off and the encapsulation of data.

It is easy to underestimate the importance of a good physical installation of a CSMA/CD LAN. Any poorly installed transceiver or damaged medium can have a serious performance effect (Leong 1985). Also of importance is the safety of the installation, particularly when cable is being taken between different buildings which may have different earth potentials. The cable can also present problems when exposed externally, as it can act as a lightning conductor. The European Computer Manufacturer's Association (ECMA 1985) have produced a useful safety guide (ECMA97), which examines these issues in detail.

7.5   SYSTEM LIMITATIONS

As noted previously, all the frames transmitted on the CSMA/CD cable must be long enough to reach the end of the cable before the sender stops sending, otherwise two complete frames could be in transit and collide without being detected. The length of the cable is determined by setting a maximum end-to-end transmission time, and is thus related to the speed of transmission and the rate of attenuation along the medium.

The first IEEE CSMA/CD standard based on the Ethernet specification runs at 10 Mbit/s, and the maximum length of a trunk coaxial segment is set at 500 m. The IEEE have adopted a naming convention under which this LAN is now referred to as *10base5*, (*10* Mbit/s, *base*-band, (5×100)m segments), to distinguish it from the other variants, described in this chapter. All the comments in 7.4 on the physical aspects of the LAN apply to 10base5 only.

7.5.1   Segment configurations
The simplest 10base5 LAN comprises a single segment of up to 500 m (Fig. 7.3), with stations attached at points at least 2.5 m apart. There is a limit of 100 transceivers on a segment, however, even though there are 200 marked attachment points. The minimum single segment arrangement can be extended by the use of *repeater sets* (a repeater plus two MAUs, normally simply referred to as a repeater), which regenerate the signal.

A repeater (Fig. 7.4) can couple together two 500 m segments of coaxial cable. The repeater occupies one transceiver position on each segment and must pass all the signals from one cable to the other, including collision jamming, thus giving the illusion that the two segments are one. Another type of medium extension is the *link segment,* where two repeater sets link one coaxial segment to a remote coaxial segment via a fibre optic point-to-

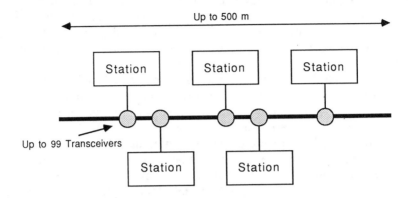

Fig. 7.3 — Single segment IEEE 802.3 LAN.

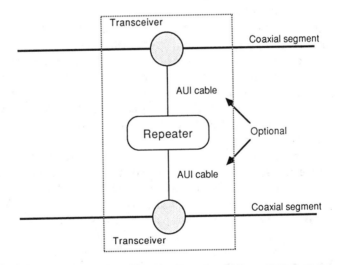

Fig. 7.4 — A coaxial to coaxial repeater.

point link segment between the repeaters. The fibre link can be up to 1 km long, but it is not possible to place a MAU on a link segment. Thus they are only useful for reaching distant corners of a site, or for traversing difficult environments where fibre optic cable is desired.

The critical limitation on extending 10base5 LANs in this way is the overall propagation time between the two furthest apart stations. The specification permits a maximum end-to-end transmission time of 44.95 microseconds. The AUIs, transceivers, coaxial segments, repeaters and link segments all contribute transmission delays and the overall limit works out to 5 segments, only three of which can be coaxial segments. Thus the maximum end-to-end configuration is as shown in Fig. 7.5. Note, however, that large networks can be devised without violating the number of segments limit between any two stations, by placing many segments off the middle coaxial segment, as shown in Fig. 7.6.

It will not always be the case that every installation will wish to use the full 500 m of each coaxial segment, and it is possible to link smaller segments, using barrel connectors, up to the limit of 500 m. Each join is a potential signal reflection point, however, and there many be significant differences in impedance between different batches of cable. Thus it is recommended that unbroken cable be used if possible, but if not, that cable from the same manufacturer and batch be used. A further recommendation, to reduce the probability of the signal adding in phase at each join, is to use lengths of cable which correspond to odd integral multiples of a half 5 MHz wavelength. Thus many cable suppliers offer lengths with the seemingly peculiar values of 23.4 m, 70.2 m and 117 m. It is very important when dealing with smaller segments to record what lengths have been used where so that accurate matching can take place.

7.5.2   10base5 extensions

Although 10base5 has been available for some time, the basic components are still relatively expensive. A controller board, transceiver and drop cable may cost more than many PCs, and are even expensive relative to minicomputers. For that reason several manufacturers market products which help to reduce costs, notably the transceiver *fan-out* box, or multi-port transceiver (Fig. 7.7). This device enables up to eight stations to be connected, and can either be used as an 8 station LAN by itself or can be attached to a normal transceiver, thus giving eight transceivers at one point. This is a useful solution where there is a high density of stations (as 2.5 m of 10base5 cable can be difficult to hide between stations), and costs less than half the cost of 8 transceivers. It is also possible, by attaching eight multi-port boxes into one box in a tree structure, to create a 64 station LAN with no actual coaxial cable in the system. It is not, however, then possible to connect such a two tier system directly to a 10base5 cable.

Finally, the fibre optic *star-coupler* or *hub* should be noted. As mentioned earlier, IEEE has drawn up a specification for a point-to-point fibre-optic link, but some manufacturers have produced star couplers which are multi-way repeaters, as illustrated in Fig. 7.8. These devices are equivalent to placing up to eight repeaters at the one point, but they do not assist in extending the LAN beyond the '5 segments' rule mentioned earlier.

7.6   THIN WIRE CSMA/CD (CHEAPERNET)

Thus far, this chapter has described the original IEEE 802.3 standard, but recently there have been several related CSMA/CD developments. The first is known as 10base2, or more commonly as *thin wire* CSMA/CD. As can be seen from the name, this version operates at 10 Mbit/s as before, and uses

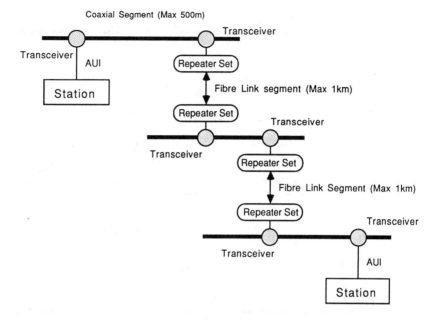

Fig. 7.5 — Example of a maximum segment configuration.

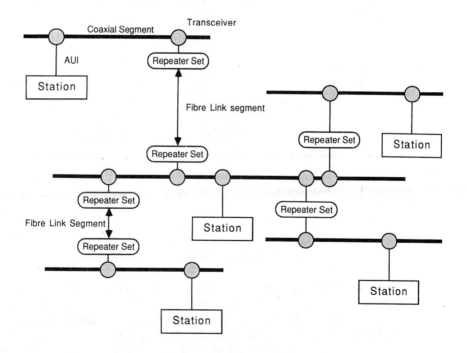

Fig. 7.6 — Example of a large multi-segment configuration.

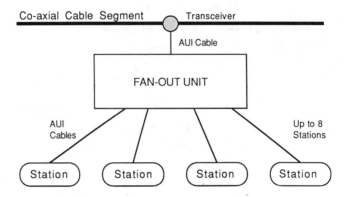

Fig. 7.7 — Typical FAN-OUT unit arrangement.

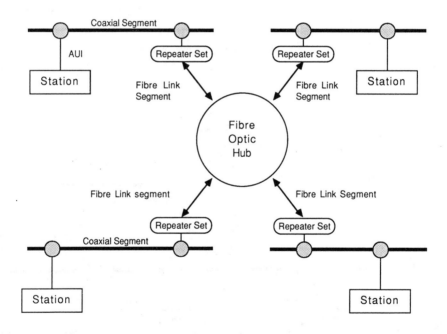

Fig. 7.8 — Example of a fibre optic hub arrangement.

the same baseband transmission, but the medium is a thinner, more flexible cable. The cable is an industry standard known as RG58, and is much cheaper than 10base5 cable. The main limitation is that the length of a segment is limited to 185 m. Because of the different cable characteristics, only 30 stations can be placed on a 10base2 segment, but the inter-station gap is reduced to 0.5 m.

The main advanatage of 10base2 is that its greater flexibility means that the cable can be taken directly to the controller board within the station. Connection to the cable is via a simple *T-piece,* elminating the need for the costly transceiver and drop cable, although stations can also be attached via a transceiver if required. The T-piece method has made it the most popular method of attaching the cheaper PCs to CSMA/CD networks, and has also gained the system the name of *cheapernet.* Although many users install CSMA/CD networks constructed entirely of 10base2 cable, it is possible to install a backbone LAN of 10base5 cable, with 10base2 segments running from it, attached via repeaters as normal. In practice, in order to make the cost even more attractive, 10base2 segments are often linked to a 10base5 cable using a *multi-port repeater,* as shown in Fig. 7.9. it is also possible to

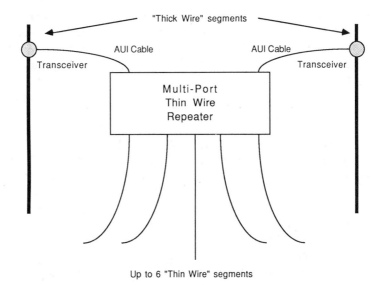

Fig. 7.9 — A typical thin wire multi-port repeater configuration.

mix thin and thick cable on the same segment, but this is not recommended.

7.7 BROADBAND CSMA/CD

A second variant, 10broad36, has also received IEEE approval. As the name implies, this is a broadband version, in which a few sets of frequencies are reserved for 10 Mbit/s CSMA/CD channels. The modems required for broadband, called *broadband transceivers,* present the normal transceiver interface to the station, and the big advantage of this technique is the 3.6 km segment limit.

Broadband transceivers operate in a different way from their baseband counterparts (Abraham 1986). Because the same controller boards are used, which send a Manchester encoded 10 Mbit/s signal to the transceiver, the signal must be narrowed or it would occupy some 80 MHz on the broadband cable. This is achieved by filtering the signal and changing the method of encoding the data. To improve the reliability further, the frame is scrambled, apart from the preamble part, which is still required for synchronisation.

On a baseband CSMA/CD network, the end of the frame is indicated by a total lack of signal on the medium. For broadband, as the carrier signal is always present, it is necessary to add a 23 bit sequence (a *postamble*) to the end of the frame. The final difference is that the baseband collision detection techniques are not applicable. Broadband transceivers can detect collisions only by seeing errors in the station's own address, i.e. the station listens to its own address on the receive channel, or the station's modem detects an incoming transmission just as the station tries to transmit, or the end of the unscrambled part of the packet fails to be detected at the correct time. The packets are so constructed that at least one of the colliding stations will detect one of the above conditions. When it does so it transmits a jamming signal in a reserved 4 Mhz wide band immediately adjacent to the 14 Mhz band used for the data itself. Thus any transmission in this band indicates a collision.

7.8   TWISTED PAIR CSMA/CD (STARLAN)

The most recent addition to the IEEE CSMA/CD stable of LANs is 1base5, which uses a tree topology and operates at 1 Mbit/s. In this system the medium used is twisted pair cable, and the repeaters are called *STARLAN hubs* (Fig. 7.10). Like the 10base2 system it is intended for linking a moderate number of PCs together at low cost. Unlike the 10base2 system, it cannot be connected directly to any of the other IEEE CSMA/CD LANs because of the transmission speed differences. Up to 64 stations can be connected in a StarLAN system, with a station being up to 250 m from its hub. Two tiers of hub are permitted, and thus a station can be up to 500 m from the base hub.

1base5 is generating a great deal of interest in North America, because unused telephone cable pairs can be used as the medium. The situation in Europe is not so encouraging as the telephone cable within a user's building usually remains the property of the PTT, and non-approved equipment cannot be attached to it.

7.9   CONCLUSION

Of all the general purpose LANs, CSMA/CD, particularly the 10base5 version, has been on the market for longest and has a very large installation base. The 10base5 standard has been adopted by the International Standards Organisation as an international standard, and the number of manufacturers offering products continues to grow. It can be expected that at least some of the other variants will also become international standards.

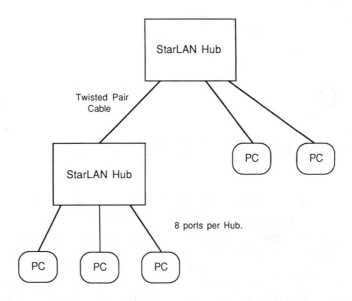

Fig. 7.10 — IEEE 802.3 1base5 (StarLAN) configuration.

IEEE continue to refine their work, and manufacturers continue to produce improved products. One can expect, for example, that the segment limitations outlined above will be relaxed as repeater technology improves, and that the cost of transceivers and controllers will fall as the standard is now stable, and thus more manufacturers are prepared to produce equipment conforming to it.

8

The IEEE 802.5 token ring

8.1 HISTORICAL BACKGROUND

One of the most important developments in local area networks over the past few years was the launch of IBM's token ring local area network in October 1985. The development work started in 1979 at IBM's Zurich Research Laboratory, and the first public announcements were made in a series of papers presented to the Institute of Electrical and Electronic Engineers Computer Society's COMPCON conference in September 1982 (Dixon 1982, Markov & Strole 1982, Andrews & Shultz 1982).

While developing the ring, IBM were active in promoting their chosen technique in the standards arena, first in the European Computer Manufacturers Association with the ECMA-89 standard, and then within the Institute of Electrical and Electronic Engineers (IEEE). This has resulted in the IEEE 802.5 standard, which is now a draft International Standard (ISO DIS 8802/5). In concert with this promotion, IBM agreed with Texas Instruments that they should produce a chip-set which would implement the specification, and which would be available to all manufacturers to incorporate in their products.

Unfortunately, the TI/IBM chip-set appears to implement rather more than is in the IEEE specification, although it is compatible with it. This has led to some claims that IBM is merely paying lip-service to the standard and that other products which comply with the standard may have some difficulty in communicating with IBM products if they do not use the Texas Instruments chips (Meir 1986). The remainder of this chapter gives details of the IEEE specification. The IBM/TI implementation is believed to include additional MAC frames, which may be concerned with the interconnection of multiple ring systems. These have not been released for public consumption as yet.

8.2 METHOD OF OPERATION

The principle of token rings was examined in Chapter 5, but to summarise: each station connects to the ring via a repeater, which takes the incoming data from the station upstream and passes it on, bit by bit, to the station downstream. The stations are connected serially by the medium in a loop (Fig. 8.1), and the data always travels in the same direction.

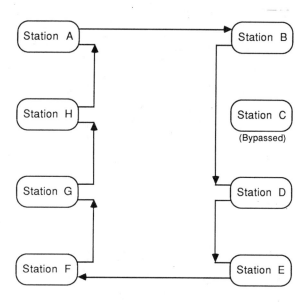

Fig. 8.1 — Token ring configuration.

To prevent multiple simultaneous access to the ring, a station must wait until a *token* arrives before it can transmit data. When a station detects a token on the ring and wishes to transmit, it changes the token into a data packet, and inserts its data. The data will be passed round the ring to the receiver who will read it, by copying it into a buffer, append a marker to indicate receipt, and pass it on round the ring back to the transmitter, who removes it from the ring. When the transmitter has finished, it puts the token back on the ring for another station to use.

Most of the complexity of the token ring involves the error recovery procedures: not simply the traditional communications problems of corrupt data, but dealing with lost tokens and multiple tokens. This is achieved by using one station as an *active monitor,* as explained below.

8.3 MEDIUM ACCESS CONTROL FRAME FORMATS

Fig. 8.2 shows the format of a frame on the token ring. The same format is used to transmit data and ring management packets, the latter being known as *Medium Access Control* (MAC) packets. The only frames which are different are the token frame and an abort frame. The fields of the frame are as follows:

Starting delimiter (SD) An 8 bit sequence to indicate the start of the frame. The sequence includes some 'bits' which violate the Manchester encoding and thus are very easy to detect. Note that no long preamble is required as in IEEE 802.3.

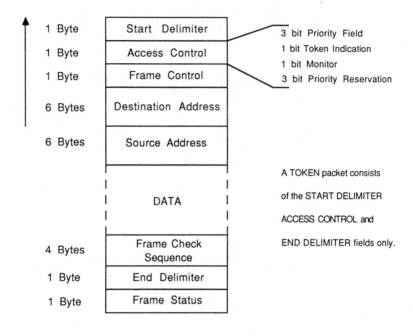

Fig. 8.2 — Token ring frame format.

Access control (AC)   This is an 8 bit field whose format is shown in Fig. 8.3. The *PPP* and *RRR* bits are concerned with the token priority scheme, explained in 8.4.3. The 'T' bit indicates when set to '1' that this is a *token frame*, which simply consists of a start delimiter field, an access control field (with the 'T' bit set to '1'), and an ending delimiter field; i.e. it is a 24 bit frame as shown in Fig. 8.4.

The 'M' bit is the *monitor* bit, and is used by the monitor station to detect a packet which has not been removed from the ring. When a station transmits a frame, the 'M' bit is set to zero. As it passes the monitor station, it is set to '1'. As the transmitting station must remove the packet when it receives it back round the loop, the monitor station should never see any packet, token or data, with the 'M' bit set to '1'. If it does, it removes the frame.

Frame control (FC)   (Refer to Fig. 8.2.) This field uses the most significant 2 bits to indicate the type of frame. '00' indicates a MAC frame, i.e. ring management, and '01' indicates a data frame (the other values are reserved for future use). For a MAC frame, the remaining bits indicate the type of management message which follows in the data field. For a data frame, the remaining bits can be used to indicate some forms of priority for the data. The different MAC frames are discussed in 8.4.

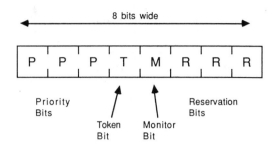

Fig. 8.3 — Format of access control field.

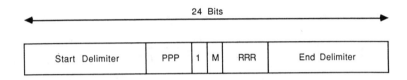

Fig. 8.4 — Format of token frame.

Destination address (DA) This field identifies the station which is to receive the data. As with the IEEE 802.3 LAN (Chapter 7, Fig. 7.2), the first bit indicates whether the address is an individual or group address, and the second bit shows if the address is globally or locally administered. In addition to reserving the 'all 1s' value as a *broadcast* address for packets intended for all stations, the token ring reserves the address 'all 0s' for packets not addressed to any particular station. This setting can occur in ring management packets.

Source address (SA) This identifies the station which transmitted the frame.

Information field (INFO) This contains the data in the case of a data frame, or a MAC *vector* if it is a MAC frame. The INFO field is subdivided further for a MAC frame as indicated in Fig. 8.5.
The basic unit of a MAC message is the *vector*, of which there can only be one in any one frame. The vector comprises a 16 bit length field, which indicates the length of the whole vector, followed by a 16 bit vector identifier. There can then follow any number of subvectors, which can be thought of as the parameters of the vector. Each subvector consists of an 8 bit length field, an 8 bit subvector identifier, and then as many bytes as are needed to convey the vector value. Some examples of these vectors are given in section 8.4. In the specifications, the lengths of fields are usually denoted

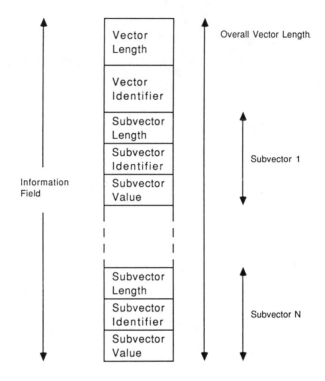

Fig. 8.5 — Format of MAC information frame.

in *octets* as some systems use bytes which are not 8 bits long, but in this book one byte is the same as one octet which is eight bits.

Note that unlike the IEEE CSMA/CD LAN, there is no mandatory minimum size to the frame (the token frame is actually the smallest at 24 bits), nor is there a maximum size to the frame. When a station has captured the token it has a certain *time* in which to utilise the ring, and it can transmit as long a frame as possible within that time period. The specification does lay down, however, that all stations must be capable of receiving frames with an information field of up to 133 octets.

Frame check sequence (FCS)   This is a 32 bit long checksum, designed to detect bit transmission errors.

Ending delimiter (ED)   Like the starting delimiter, this is a unique pattern which violates the Manchester encoding, and is thus easy to detect. The final two bits have special significance, however: the *intermediate frame bit* is set to '1' to indicate that this frame is not the last frame of a multiple frame transmission, and is set to '0' if it is the last frame. The second, known as the *error-detected bit* is set to '0' by the station which originates the frame. All the stations have an obligation to check for errors, by using the frame check sequence for example, and if they detect an error they set this bit to '1'.

Frame status field (FS)   The final 8 bits of the frame are used to determine if the receiving station exists on the ring, and whether it was able to copy the frame or not.

The format of this field is given in Fig. 8.6. Because it is transmitted *after*

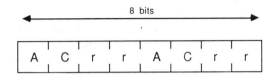

A = Address recognised, C = Frame Copied, r = reserved

Fig. 8.6 — Frame status field format.

the checksum field, and therefore is not checked by it, the two significant bits, A and C, are transmitted twice within the field. The originating station sets both bits to '0'. The receiver uses the A bit, to indicate *address recognised*, i.e. if the frame returns to the originator with this bit still set to '0', then the destination station was not present on the ring. The C bit, *frame copied*, is used by the receiving station to indicate that the frame was good and was copied successfully into the receiver's buffer.

8.4   RING MANAGEMENT

It is easy to see from the foregoing how the ring operates in a steady state condition and how simple transmission errors are dealt with. The major problems with ring systems, however, are in initialisation of the ring, i.e. in starting the token, and in dealing with lost or corrupt tokens. In some ring systems, notably the Cambridge ring, there is a monitor station expressly for this purpose. This adds to the cost of the system, especially as the monitor station may have to be duplicated for resilience. In the IEEE token ring, every station has the capability of being the monitor station. One station is the *active monitor*. It ensures that the token does not get lost and it deals with permanently circulating frames. It also maintains the clocking rate of the ring, keeping all the stations synchronised with each other.

The active monitor also contains a *latency buffer*, whereby instead of repeating each bit as it goes past, the monitor stores each bit and introduces a delay into the ring. This serves two purposes. First, the ring must be physically long enough to hold the 24 bit token when all the stations are idle. In a small ring the cable may not be long enough for this, and so the latency buffer is made 24 bits long so that even a two station ring will work correctly.

The second purpose of the latency buffer is to compensate for *phase jitter*. The active monitor provides a master clock rate for all the stations on the ring, and each station should track the frequency and phase of this signal. However, in practice there are slight speed and phase differences on each leg of the ring, and in the worst case they can cause variations of up to plus or minus 3 bit times. Unless these are compensated for, bits are either lost or gained on each lap. Thus the 24 bit latency buffer is set to 27 bits, and the active monitor will use between 24 and 30 bits of latency to compensate for the ring speed, more than 27 to avoid losing bits, or less than 27 to avoid gaining bits.

Meanwhile all the other stations are monitoring the active monitor station in a *standby* mode. It transmits an *Active Monitor Present (AMP)* MAC frame at regular intervals and this is used for two distinct purposes: to allow the standby stations to check that the active monitor is working, and to permit stations to determine who their neighbour is by a scheme called *neighbour notification*.

8.4.1 Neighbour notification and beaconing

One of the useful features of a ring system is that, because the stations have distinct transmission paths between them, a station which receives a faulty packet knows that it must have been caused by its upstream neighbour. The token ring uses a system called *beaconing*, in which a station detecting such an error will send a 'beacon' MAC frame to all the stations on the ring, including the faulty one, which warns them that the ring service is suspended. When a station sees a beacon frame concerning itself, it has to assume that it is faulty and will isolate itself from the ring. The physical mechanism for this is explained below. The beaconing system also means that any ring monitoring software can quickly report problems to the appropriate operations staff. The beacon MAC frame is an interesting example of the MAC frame format discussed above; it is shown in Fig. 8.7.

As can be seen, the crucial parameter required is the address of the station upstream of the station reporting the error; this is sent as subvector 1 of the beacon frame. The *neighbour notification* scheme allows each station to find out which is its upstream neighbour, as follows.

The Active Monitor *broadcasts* — destination address set to 'all stations' — an *Active Monitor Present (AMP)* frame, with the address recognised A bit and frame copied C bit of the frame status field both set to '0' as normal (Fig. 8.8 (a)). The first station to receive this will store the active monitor's address, since this is its upstream neighbour, and set the A bit to '1'. The frame will then be seen by all the other stations on the ring, but they will merely note that the Active Monitor is still operational.

Meanwhile, as a result of detecting the active monitor present frame, the first station gets ready to send a *Standby Monitor Present (SMP)* frame, which it does when it next gets the token (Fig. 8.8 (b)). In the same way as before the next station will be the only one which sees the SMP frame with the A and the C bits set to '0', and will know that the frame has come from its immediate upstream neighbour. The other stations all ignore SMP frames with the A and C bits set to one. As each station sees an SMP frame from its neighbour it in turn transmits an SMP frame of its own. This continues round

Field Name	Value	Comment
Frame Control	00 000010	MAC frame intended for all to action
Destination Address	All 1's	All stations on the ring
Source Address	as required	The station which has detected the fault
Vector Length	X'0F'	Including its own length of 2 bytes
Vector Identifier	X'0002'	BEACON
Subvector 1 Length	X'08'	Includes its own length of 1 byte
Subvector 1 Identifier	X'02'	RUA (Received Upstream Neighbour)
Subvector 1 Value	as required	Address of RUA (6 bytes)
Subvector 2 Length	X'04'	
Subvector 2 Identifier	X'01'	Beacon Type
Subvector 2 Value	as required	Depends on circumstances when the error was detected.

(Note : X'...' means the value between the quotes is in hexadecimal)

Fig. 8.7 — Format of BEACON MAC frame.

the ring until the active monitor sees an SMP frame with the A and C bits set to '0', at which point every station knows who its upstream neighbour is. In practice each station waits for a certain time before sending the SMP frame to prevent the ring being loaded with consecutive SMPs.

8.4.2   Active monitor recovery

Each standby station, i.e. every station apart from the active monitor station, maintains a timer to check that an AMP frame is received within a certain time. Each station also checks that a token frame passes by within a certain time. If either of these times is exceeded, the station assumes that the active monitor has failed and it starts to send *transmit claim token* frames. This is the only area of ring access where there may be some contention, as several stations may attempt to become the active monitor simultaneously.

This is resolved by each station examining the source address of any incoming claim token frame. If the station's own address is numerically higher than that of the station which originated the claim token frame, then it removes the claim token frame and substitutes its own. Once its own packet has come back round it can assume that it is the new active monitor. A station which assumes an active monitor role will revert to standby if it sees either an active monitor present frame, or a *purge* frame (which is used to reset the ring), which it did not itself originate. Thus there should be no possibility of duplicate active monitors on a ring.

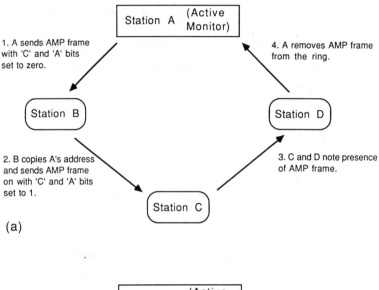

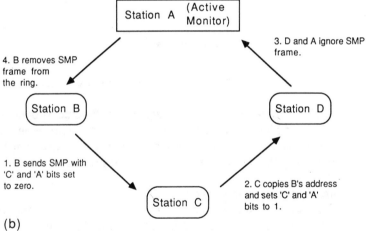

Fig. 8.8 — Active and standby monitor functions.

8.4.3   Token priority system

A further important feature of the token ring is its use of priorities, mentioned in the description of the AC field above. Each frame carries a three bit priority field, PPP, which indicates the priority level of the data or token being carried. The ring always starts with tokens of the lowest priority, '000' ('111' is the highest). The priority system can be used to guarantee access to the medium for certain categories of data, for example synchronous or real-time information.

The priority system is best illustrated by example. Assume that station B is already transmitting at the priority level of '1' to station D, and station A has a message of priority '4' which it wishes to send to station C (Fig. 8.9 (a)).

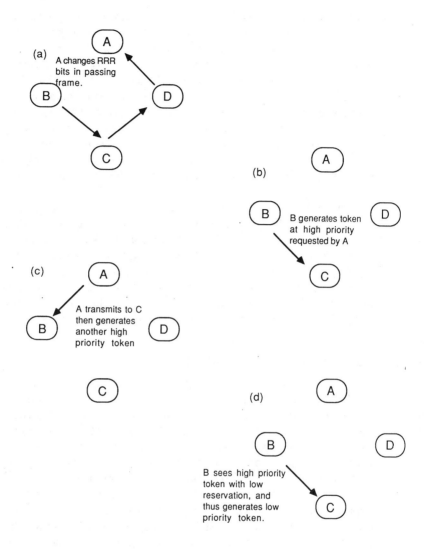

Fig. 8.9 — Example of priority system.

Station A sets the reservation bits (RRR) in the AC field of the passing data frame to the value '4', assuming that the current RRR bits are not higher than '4' — i.e. assuming that no other station has meanwhile placed an even higher priority reservation. When station B generates the new token (Fig. 8.9(b)), it must be set to the priority requested by the RRR bits ('4'), with the RRR bits reset to zero. Stations can only use the token to send data with that priority or higher, and in this way there is fair access for all the data at the same priority.

Once a station has raised the priority of the data on the ring, as station B has done, it becomes a *stacking* station. It must remember the priority level the ring was at before it raised it ('1' in this case), and the level to which it has just been raised. It does this by recording the information in two *stacks*, one for the current level and one for the old level. It must then examine every token generated at or above the new priority level, to see if the priority can be lowered again. In the example, once A has finished transmitting to C, it generates a token with the PPP bits set to the current priority ('4'), and with the RRR bits set to zero (Fig. 8.9(c)), unless a further reservation has been made by another station or A itself has some further data to send but has run out of time. The stacking station will lower the priority of the passing token if the RRR bits are not greater than the value stacked as the previous level ('1'); i.e. if no other station has reserved the token at a priority level higher than the stacking station has remembered the previous level to be (Fig. 8,9(d)).

   If another station has requested a priority token, at level '3' for example, the stacking station replaces the '4' on top of the stack with a '3' and generates a level '3' token. It is still that stacking station's responsibility to reduce the priority to its original level ('1' in this case) whenever it can, i.e. whenever there are no higher priority reservations. The process is called stacking because a single station may raise the priority of the ring more than once before it gets lowered, e.g. from 0 to 3, then 3 to 6. It thus has to remember each level on a stack, to lower the priority gradually.

8.5   PHYSICAL COMPONENTS

Physically, a token ring consists of *Trunk Coupling Units* (TCUs), linked by trunk cables. A station connects to its TCU via a *medium interface cable*, which can be in two parts, the station connecting to a wall socket, and the wall socket wired to the TCU (Fig. 8.10). Both the interface cable and the trunk cables are two shielded twisted pairs. All of the repeater function, address recognition and MAC frame activities take place on the controller board in the station, and thus the interface cable is very much part of the ring. The TCU contains the mechanism for inserting a station into the ring or bypassing the station from the ring. A station is inserted when it has powered up and performed the self tests mentioned below. It can signal the TCU to take it physically out of the ring, whenever the beaconing system is operated.

   IBM's implementation, based on their Common Cabling System, is to group the TCUs into wiring concentrators, called Multi-station Access Units, with a loop of cable from a concentrator out to each station. Each concentrator has 8 ports and the concentrators are connected together to form the ring (Fig. 8.11). In this way the ring can be positioned in a convenient location, for example the basement of a building, and the stations can be scattered throughout the building. The concentrators also provide a convenient way of isolating parts of the ring if necessary, and adding or removing stations is simple and almost nondisruptive.

   As mentioned above, when a station powers up, it goes through a self-test procedure with its wiring concentrators, passing some 1500 packets to itself before being allowed onto the ring. A station bringing itself onto or off

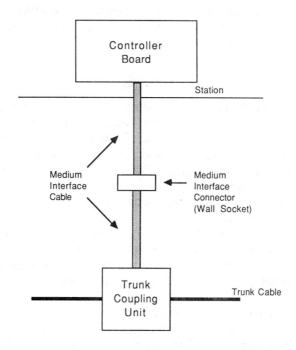

Fig. 8.10 — Station to cable coupling schematic.

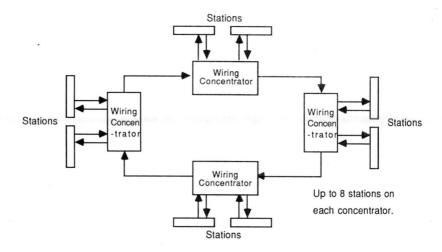

Fig. 8.11 — Wiring concentrator system.

the ring in practice causes some disruption to data traffic on the ring, but this is unlikely to be a problem unless many stations power on or off simultaneously.

8.6   SYSTEM LIMITATIONS

The current version of the token ring operates at 4 Mbit/s, although one may expect this to increase in the future. The main system limitation is the limit to the number of stations. Using full specification twisted pair cable the limit is set at 260 stations, as this is the point at which the phase jitter problem becomes nonrecoverable. This number is dependent on the medium, and when ordinary telephone twisted pair is used the number falls to 72, although this may also place other distance restrictions on the LAN (Bates & Abramson 1986).

The distance that any station can be from an IBM wiring concentrator depends on the configuration, but is typically no more than 100 m. The concentrators themselves can be up to 200 m apart, or 750 m using additional repeaters. Distances of up to 2 km are also achievable by using fibre optic cable.

In conclusion, the token ring is certain to be a major force in local area networks over the next few years. IBM are known to be working on various enhancements, including a fibre optic version; and bridges, gateways and many compatible LANs will appear.

9

IEEE 802.4 token bus network

9.1 INTRODUCTION

The token bus LAN (IEEE 802.4,ISO DIS 8802/4) is the third of the major specifications to emerge from the IEEE project 802, and in many ways is both the most complex and the most specialised in terms of the end users who may wish to use it.

It has been backed mainly by those involved in factory networks, who desire the simplicity of a bus network, but also the guaranteed maximum delivery times of a token passing network. CSMA/CD, for example, is a non-deterministic access system, as it is not possible to predict the time it will take for a frame to be transmitted between any two stations. With token passing systems, a maximum delivery time can be guaranteed under normal working conditions, and this is important for some applications, for example process control. The main user base of the token bus is provided by systems which have adopted the MAP (Manufacturer Automation Protocol) suite of protocols, which is discussed in Chapter 16.

9.2 METHOD OF OPERATION

Once the network has reached a steady state, i.e. when the stations have been organised into a logical ring, the token bus works in a similar way to the token ring of the previous chapter, with a station only able to transmit when it has obtained the token. Because the stations are on a broadcast type of network, however, and the transmissions reach the whole length of the bus, there is no need for the stations to repeat the data, as in the ring. The token passing mechanism requires that the stations be organised into a logical ring, as shown in Fig. 9.1. Thus the logical sequence in Fig. 9.1 is A–F–C–E–B. One advantage of the token bus system is that a station can receive all transmitted frames without being in the logical token passing ring; for example station D in Fig. 9.1. This can be useful for network management and for telemetry systems, where a station need only monitor a system, without itself sending any data on the LAN.

A token bus offers two other advantages over other systems. First it is *in principle* possible to insert a station more than once into the logical token ring, thus implementing a priority scheme, although the IEEE system in fact uses the station addresses to enforce the logical sequence. Secondly, it is

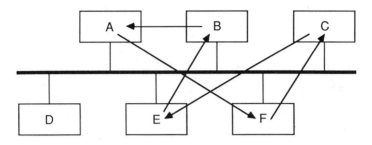

(D is not in the logical ring.)

Fig. 9.1 — Example of logical ring on the bus.

possible for a station, once it has gained the token, to use a completely different communication system to access other systems, within its turn, provided, obviously, that it does not confuse any other station. Thus it is possible to have a master station which must poll remote devices on the same cable, with only the master station within the token passing scheme, and the remote stations only aware of the master station's existence. This can lead to much simpler hardware and software in the slave stations.

As with the token ring, there is no single monitoring station in a token bus system, as all the stations are responsible for token management. In addition, however, every station is also responsible for the attachment and detachment of stations from the active logical ring. The technique by which this is achieved is described later in the chapter.

9.3   MEDIUM ACCESS CONTROL FRAME FORMATS

As might be expected, the token bus frame format, shown in Fig. 9.2, has some of the features of both the CSMA/CD bus (Fig. 7.1) and the token ring (Fig. 8.2). The elements are as follows:

Preamble   This is a constant bit pattern, designed to let the receivers synchronise with the transmitter. The number of octets depends on the speed of the LAN (several speeds over a variety of media are permitted in the specification), but the preamble must last for at least 2 microseconds.

Start delimiter   This octet defines the start of the frame.

Frame control field   This octet determines what type of frame is being sent. There are two classes, medium access control and data frames. Fig. 9.3 shows a medium access control frame, with the first two bits set to '0', and the rest interpreted as the type of control frame. The token frame itself, for example, is defined as '00001000'. The other types of control frame are concerned with the maintenance of the logical ring, and are described in the following sections. Data frames are signified by a control field as in Fig. 9.4.

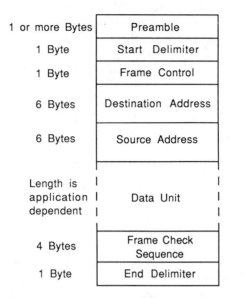

Fig. 9.2 — Token bus frame format.

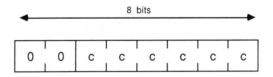

CCCCCC = Type of MAC Control frame

Fig. 9.3 — Frame control field format (MAC control frame).

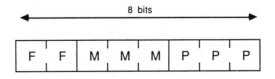

FF   = Frame Type (LLC or Station Management)
MMM   = MAC Action
PPP   = Priority

Fig. 9.4 — Frame control field format (data frame).

The first two bits can either be '01' for a normal data frame or '10' for a station management data frame. As in the token ring there are three priority bits, but note that they define the priority of the data, not of the token, and there is no reservation system. The priority system is described below. The other bits in the frame control field are reserved for possible future use.

Address fields   (Refer to Fig. 9.2) The destination address and source address fields are identical to the IEEE 802.3 (7.3) and IEEE 802.5 (8.3) address fields.

Data unit field   This contains the actual data. There is an overall frame size upper limit of 8191 octets.

Frame check sequence   This is a 32 bit checking sequence to guard against transmission errors.

End delimiter   This is a one octet pattern to signal the end of the frame. Two of the bits have significance: one is used to indicate if any more frames are about to follow from that station, and one is used as an error bit to indicate that there was a Frame Check Sequence (FCS) error. Both of these bits are used only by repeaters whose purpose is to extend the physical length of the LAN.

9.4   MEDIUM ACCESS MANAGEMENT

This section examines the procedures for the management of faults, the addition and removal of stations from the logical ring, initialisation of the network, and the priority scheme. The essence of the scheme is that each station knows the address of its two immediate neighbours in the logical ring — its predecessor and its successor — and the token is passed in descending numerical order of address. A *slot time* is defined, of equal value for all stations, which is the maximum time a station need wait for an immediate response from another station. This timeout system is used to determine and recover from errors.

9.4.1   Failed stations

Whenever a station passes the token onto the next station in the sequence, it listens for up to four slot times to hear if the next station is active, i.e. it tries to receive whatever the next station transmits. If the next station sends a valid frame, then all is well. If the station hears a frame with a checksum fault or a noise burst, it cannot be certain that the next station has the token, and so it listens again and if it hears anything else, even another faulty frame, it assumes that the next station does have the token. If it hears nothing, it sends the token again, and then waits once more. If it hears nothing again, it assumes that the next station has failed and it starts the error recovery procedure, as shown in Fig. 9.5.

The station which has detected the failure sends a *WHO FOLLOWS* control frame, which carries the address of the old successor station in the data field. All of the other stations compare that address with the address which they know is their predecessor. One station only will find a match—the station which follows the failed station. It records its new predecessor as the station which has detected the error (Fig. 9.5(b)), and it alone responds to the *WHO FOLLOWS* frame with a *SET SUCCESSOR* frame, which tells the detecting station that it now has a new successor. Thus the failed station is removed from the logical ring.

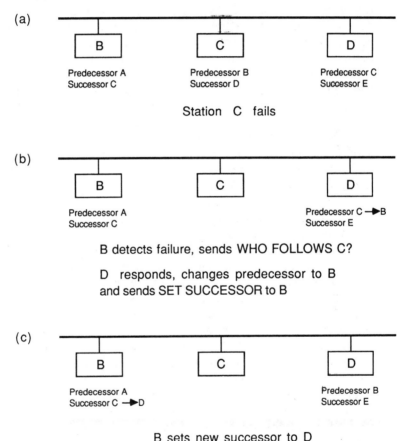

Fig. 9.5 — Example of ring reconfiguration after station failure.

It may happen, however, that no response to the *WHO FOLLOWS* frame is elicited. In this case the detecting station sends a *SOLICIT SUCCESSOR 2* frame, with its own address as both the source and destination address. This requests any station which is active and which wishes to be in the logical ring to reply, and the response windows mechanism, described below, then comes into play. If that fails, the station assumes that it itself is faulty, or that there has been a catastrophic failure of the bus, or that it is the only station left in the ring. It then enters a state of waiting until it can detect some other activity on the bus before trying again to re-establish the logical ring.

9.4.2   Response windows

The *response window* mechanism is the means by which new stations are added to the ring, and as noted above is also used under certain failure conditions. A response window is a delay of one time slot, during which a station which has sent a *SOLICIT SUCCESSOR* frame must wait for a response. The station sending such a frame specifies, in the source and destination fields of the frame, the address range of stations which are permitted to respond. In the case described above, where the source and destination addresses were equal, any station could respond.

In the normal case, a station will be trying to find any new stations between itself and its current successor whose address is lower than its own. It thus sends a *SOLICIT SUCCESSOR 1* frame, and only stations with addresses between the soliciting station and its successor can respond. If a valid response is heard, the sending station changes its successor station address and sends it the token (Fig. 9.6(a)). Eventually, the new station will forward the token to its successor, which will note that it has received the token from a new predecessor.

There are two special cases to be dealt with. First there must be one station whose successor's address is greater than its own in order to complete the logical ring. There could, therefore, be stations with addresses lower than its own and stations with addresses greater than its successor, both of which lie between the station and its successor in the ring. To overcome this, a special *SOLICIT SUCCESSOR 2* frame, which has two response windows following it, is used. Stations with an address below that of the sender must respond in the first window, and those with an address higher than its successor in the second window.

The second special case is when more than one station whose address lies within the valid range wishes to enter the ring, and thus a station gets multiple responses to the solicitation. This will be seen as noise, and so the station enters a complex arbitration scheme. Briefly, the station sends a *RESOLVE CONTENTION* frame and waits for four slot times. The competing stations are permitted to respond in only one of the slots, depending on a few bits of their address. If they hear anything while listening to the slots before the one they are allowed to respond in, they do not respond themselves, and they give up trying to enter the ring at this time. If they do not hear anything they do respond. This could still result in a collision within the one slot, but repeated *RESOLVE CONTENTION* frames, with the stations modifying their slot times, will gradually eliminate the competing stations, and yield a single successor.

The mechanism for soliciting new stations into the sequence should in theory be performed by every station every time it is about to pass the token on to the next station. This could lead to very long token rotation times, however, and so each station measures the token rotation time, i.e. the time

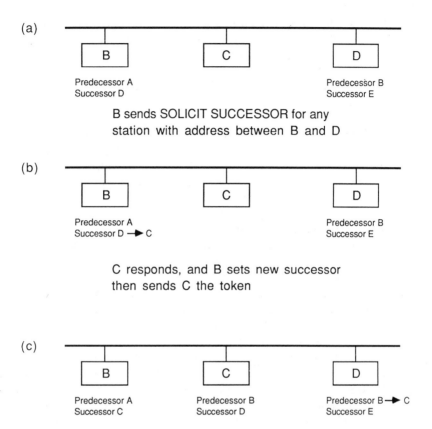

Fig. 9.6 — Example of station entering the logical ring.

since it last saw a token, and only if this is less than some preset value determined by the network manager does the station invoke the solicitation procedure. Thus on a very busy network, new stations may be prevented from entering the ring for a considerable time.

9.4.3 Initialisation
The initialisation of the logical ring is treated as a special case of adding new stations, with the difference that a *CLAIM TOKEN* frame is used by the first active station in order to start the ring up. This mechanism is invoked after an inactivity timeout has expired.

Again it could be that two stations simultaneously try to initialise the ring. In this case the length of the *CLAIM TOKEN* frame is determined by two bits of the address of the station, and a station must listen for a slot time to see if any other longer transmissions are taking place. If so, the station assumes that another station will initiate the first sending of a token, and it can join the ring using the soliciting method outlined above. A station trying to start up the ring will repeatedly send claim token frames, the length being altered each time using an algorithm based on a few bits of the station's address, until the whole address has been used. On each turn, only stations transmitting the longest frames will remain until one station is safe in assuming that it has control of the token.

A station can remove itself from the ring simply by ignoring the token and letting the error recovery scheme take effect, but a more efficient method is to use a *SET SUCCESSOR* frame in which a station passes to its predecessor the address of its successor, which will then become the new successor of the preceding station.

9.4.4   The priority scheme

Unlike the token ring priority system described in the previous chapter, the token bus system applies priorities to the *data* being transmitted, rather than to the *token*. There are four different levels of priority, and each station maintains four queues of frames, one for each priority level. The priority scheme is optional, however, with stations not operating it being deemed to be working at the highest priority.

The overall objective of the scheme is to allocate all of the bandwidth of the system to the high priority frames, only transmitting the lower priority ones if there is sufficient bandwidth. This works by each station measuring the time it takes the token to go round the 'ring', a measure which is already made for use in the 'new station solicitation scheme' described above. Each priority level has a preset target *token rotation time*, and only if this target time is bettered can a station transmit frames at that priority level.

To prevent any one station monopolising the network, there is another timer which limits the time during which that station can hold the token. Thus when a station receives the token, it can transmit any high priority frames it has, so long as it does not exceed its time. If it has time left it can start on the next lowest priority queue, but only if the target rotation time for that queue has been bettered. It can then go down to the subsequent queues in turn, again only if its overall time slot has not been exceeded and each target time for the token rotation has been bettered. In this way the overall load on the system regulates the priority of the frames which may be transmitted, with high priority frames always getting a good share of the LAN.

9.5   PHYSICAL COMPONENTS

There are three different media defined within the token bus specification, depending on the user's requirements. Each uses a different topology, employs different data encoding techniques, and runs at different speeds.

The first is a simple linear bus, using 75-Ω cable, with station attachment being via very short 'stub' cables. It uses Manchester encoding and a form of frequency shift keying termed *phase continuous*, in which the translations between signalling frequencies are performed by a continuous change of frequency rather than a step change. It operates a single channel at 1 Mbit/s, modulated onto a single frequency.

The second is also a broadband network, using a different form of frequency shift keying called *phase coherent* — the frequency changes are made when the carrier signal has a zero voltage — and offering a choice of frequencies, depending on the speed required. It operates over a tree structured topology, but with no active headend, and can be run at 5 Mbit/s or 10 Mbit/s.

Unlike the first two, the third version offers multiple channel operation, over a full broadband network, with speeds of either 1 Mbit/s, 5 Mbit/s or 10 Mbit/s.

In conclusion, the token bus has been targeted at very specialist areas, particularly the factory network, where guaranteed response times are paramount. Their market share is very low, but the advent of the MAP protocols, discussed in Chapter 16, could make this type of LAN increasingly important in the next few years.

PART 4
Protocols and standards

Part 3 has described the hardware elements of some major local area networks currently available. The physical and medium access control (MAC) rules have been enshrined in standard specifications, and thus many equipment manufacturers are developing products with hardware interfaces to at least one of those LANs, in particular the CSMA/CD LAN, which has been on the market longest.

The fact that two computers can physically attach to a LAN cable and send frames to each other over that cable does not, however, necessarily imply that one can meaningfully transfer information to the other. There has to be some agreement as to the interpretation of the contents of the frames, so that end user applications, such as file transfer and electronic mail, can be implemented. The ability to communicate is termed *connectivity*, and it is achieved by the definition of a set of communication *protocols*.

A protocol is a set of rules governing the interchange of data between two entities, and the MAC rules described in the previous section are examples of low level protocols. Most manufacturers have developed their own protocols for communication between their own equipment, e.g. ICL's CO3 and IBM's 3270 for interactive terminal to mainframe access. Many of these protocols have been incorporated into suites of protocols for general communications, for example IBM's Systems Network Architecture (SNA), and these have been published so that other manufacturers can adopt them also. Thus communication between some different manufacturers' equipment has been available by using these de facto standards.

This part first examines international communications standards and how they relate to LANs, then describes two of the most popular de facto LAN protocols, and finally addresses the particular problems of PC software for LANs.

10

The ISO open systems reference model

10.1 OPEN SYSTEMS INTERCONNECTION

Over the past few years there has been considerable effort expended on tackling the problem of interworking between different manufacturers' equipment, by defining standard protocols which *all* manufacturers can agree to implement. The pressure for such standardisation has come from three main sources.

First, the large end user has been faced with considerable problems when trying to connect equipment bought from different manufacturers. In many cases the user has not bought the system otherwise best suited to the application, simply because it could not communicate with his existing systems. Secondly, many of the manufacturers see the utilisation of de facto standards, in particular IBM's SNA protocols, as handing too large an advantage to IBM. It can also place the manufacturers in a difficult position if IBM choose to alter a protocol, in that there can be a gap of some months, if not years, before they can catch up. Finally, the PTTs (Postal, Telegraph & Telephone companies), who provide the national carrier networks in most countries, are also keen to promote standards, to increase the probability of all users using one large network run by the PTTs, rather than have them set up different private networks.

The implementation of standard protocols can bring many benefits to the end user and the manufacturer. For example:

- Users can choose their new equipment in the knowledge that it will work with the old, even if from a different supplier.
- This in turn will produce healthier competition from manufacturers, who will have to sell their systems purely on their suitability for the user's application, and thus reduce prices.
- The lifetime of a system will be extended because its communications protocols will not become redundant.
- Communication between different organisations for such activities as electronic mail and electronic funds transfer will be easier, particularly when the PTTs offer standard interfaces.
- The end user will not require multiple devices in order to communicate with multiple systems.

- All manufacturers will be encouraged to support such standards to improve the marketability of their products.

Given the number of different types of communication required to support the variety of user applications, from electronic mail to interactive terminal traffic, it has become clear that one set of protocols will not suffice, and also that some sort of structure is required so that standards can more easily be defined. The structure most commonly referred to is the *International Standards Organisation's (ISO) Open Systems Interconnection (OSI) Reference Model,* the (in)famous '7 layers', sometimes referred to as the ISORM.

Open systems interconnection is essentially the same as connectivity: the ability of any *open* system to communicate with any other *open* system (a definition of an open system is deferred to 10.3). Before describing the model, it is relevant to examine the role of the various bodies who formulate the standards.

10.2   THE STANDARDS MAKERS

There are many organisations involved in the definition of communications protocols, and in many cases they are working on the same set of standards. Fig. 10.1 shows how they relate to the two most important bodies, the

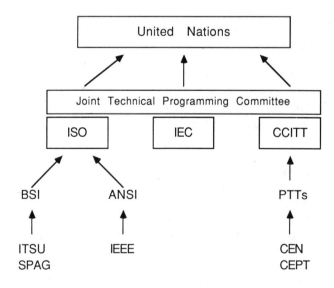

Fig. 10.1 — Relationships of standardisation organisations.

International Standards Organisation (ISO) and the International Telephone and Telegraph Consultative Committee (CCITT), which all come under the United Nations. Also shown is the International Electrotechnical Commission (IEC), which is of equivalent status to ISO but which covers such items as process control and audio/visual systems; some LANs do come within its remit, however. To coordinate the overlapping activities of these three organisations there is a Joint Technical Programming Committee, within which an Information Technology Group is responsible for aspects of computing.

ISO is a large voluntary body, consisting of some 164 technical groups, 646 subcommittees and 1585 working groups, and to date it has published over 6000 international standards covering many diverse subjects (Rankine 1986). One of the technical groups, TG97, is responsible for Information Processing Systems. This very large group, which covers not only communications but such items as magnetic tapes and character sets, is further split into sub-committees and working groups, each of which examines different aspects of the problem, and eventually produces standards documents.

The main input to ISO comes from the standards organisations of individual countries, e.g. the British Standards Institution (BSI) and the American National Standards Institute (ANSI), which make recommendations for standards to be adopted. ISO standards start off as working Draft Proposals (DP), then progress to Draft International Standards (DIS) and finally to International Standards (IS). At each stage, Addenda (ADD), Draft Addenda (DAD) or even Proposed Draft Addenda (PDAD) may be added. Each proposal is given a number which is qualified with one of the above mnemonics to indicate its status. The Appendix gives a list of the most relevant standards for LANs. To progress from one stage to the next there is a voting system, with each member country having one vote. Because these are often large, technically complex documents, and each country is entitled to comment on them, it can take many years before a standard is stable enough for a manufacturer to make a product conforming to it.

The main technical input to ISO comes from other organisations which feed into the national standards bodies. These can be national organisations themselves, for example the UK's Information Technology Standards Unit (ITSU), or more typically multinational groupings, such as the European Computer Manufacturers' Association (ECMA) and the Institute of Electrical and Electronic Engineers (IEEE). As the IEEE have been the main developer of LAN protocols, their organisation is discussed further below.

Parallel to this activity is the CCITT, which is equivalent to ISO but is concerned with telephony and public data networks. Its input is from the PTTs of individual countries, each of which is represented within it. The CCITT has produced the 'X' series of standards, of which the best known are X.25 and X.400 (Message Handling). In practice the ISO and CCITT standards tend to merge over time, with one adopting the other's standard in a given area.

In addition, there are many other groupings which both initiate and comment upon the standards. In Europe, the European Economic

Community has several, notably CEN, the group of the national standards bodies, CEPT, the group of national PTTs, and CENELEC, the group of national electro-technical committees. There are also manufacturer groupings, such as the Standards Promotion and Application Group (SPAG), and user groupings, some of which are discussed in Chapter 16.

As this much simplified description of the standards makers shows, there are many organisations involved in defining standards. One publication, for example, lists some 50 pages of standards numbers, committees and organisations with their interrelationships (Institute of Electrical Engineering 1986). As each organisation has its own numbering system this can be very confusing indeed, especially as the common usage in the literature for referring to protocols tends to be the nomenclature of whoever published the first draft of the specification. For example, most of the LAN protocol work for layers 1 and 2 was done by the IEEE Project 802 committee, and thus is known as 802.3, 802.4, etc.

10.3   THE OPEN SYSTEMS INTERCONNECTION REFERENCE MODEL

Open systems interconnection is aimed at the interworking of distributed computer applications. *Open* means that any two systems conforming to the set of standards defined by ISO should be able to communicate with each other. One of the first tasks which ISO TG97 set itself in the mid 1970s was to design a framework for the definition of the standards, and the result is the Open Systems Interconnection Reference Model (Fig. 10.2). The OSI

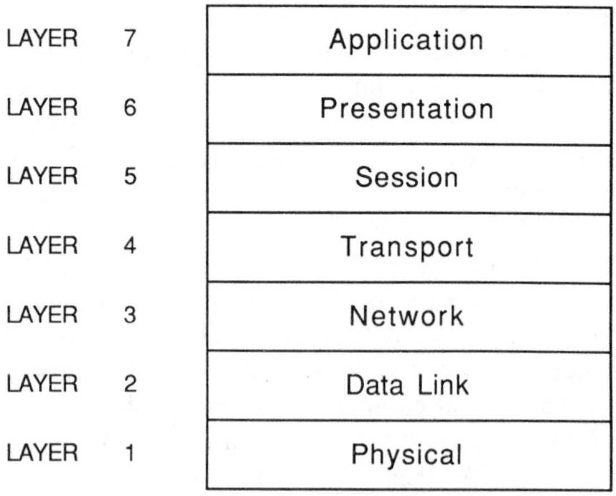

LAYER	7	Application
LAYER	6	Presentation
LAYER	5	Session
LAYER	4	Transport
LAYER	3	Network
LAYER	2	Data Link
LAYER	1	Physical

Fig. 10.2 — The ISO Open Systems Interconnection Reference Model.

model and the service definitions and protocol specifications associated with it are complex, and difficult to explain in a precise manner. The following is a brief introduction — the reader is referred to Henshall & Shaw (1988) for a comprehensive description. The OSI model introduces the important concept of *layering*. Rather than having one enormous protocol to handle all aspects of computer communications, the problem is split up into a hierarchy of layers, with each layer performing a subset of the functions required to communicate. This can be compared to structuring a computer program hierarchically using nested subroutines in the following manner.

When a team of programmers is required to produce a large complex piece of software, the problem is usually divided, and sub-divided, into logical parts or modules, each of which performs a well defined task. Each module, usually a program subroutine or set of subroutines, is given a name by which the other parts may reference it, and a specification is written to define its interface with the rest of the program.

Consider, for example, a user at the keyboard of a PC who wishes to access a record within a database held on the PC's discs. The system will probably comprise a keyboard handling routine; a syntax handler to decode the user's commands; a database application to action the user's command; a disc handler to access the required disc records; a formatter to arrange the data in the record for presentation to the screen; and finally a VDU handler to display the result. Each user access requires information to be passed through each module in the system in a predefined manner — a hierarchical system — yet each module can be designed and implemented independently.

The programmer who is writing one of the modules does not need to know *how* the other modules perform their tasks, but only what information must be presented to any module, and what information will be returned by that module. How the tasks are performed by a module will be the subject of another specification. The main advantage of this *top-down* approach is that the total problem can be tackled first, with subsequent more detailed definitions and specifications of each task being addressed separately. Note that at the first stage of allocating tasks to modules, the method of passing the information to and from the module is not defined: that is specific to the implementation and will be different for each computer system for which the program is written.

This was precisely the approach taken by ISO — to split the problem into independently manageable parts within a hierarchical structure (layers), and produce two specifications for each layer. The first, termed the *service definition*, defines the interface to the other layers and the tasks to be performed by the layer. The details of how a layer performs the task, for example how data is passed between layers, is *not* defined; such information is implementation-specific.

Each layer in the model provides a set of *services* for the layer above, and expects the layer below to provide more basic services for it. In this way the higher layers require no detailed knowledge of how the lower layers work; for example, an electronic mail program does not need to know if it is using a token ring or a CSMA/CD bus or a wide area network. Layering also means that implementation changes to one layer should not affect other layers, as the interface between the layers — *what* passes, not *how* — is fixed by the standard. Each of the higher layers of the model conceptually embraces all of the open systems on the network, e.g. there is in the model one single applications environment covering every system in the network rather than a series of application environments which happen to communicate with each other. A layer is *implemented* within a system by a layer *entity*.

The problem faced by the OSI designers, which the programming team of the analogy above do not have, is the need to coordinate activities with the system at the other end of the communications link. There is little point, for example, in transmitting a large file to a remote system unless it is able to accept and store it. All of the layers in the model require to exchange information with their corresponding layer in the remote system (or in an intermediate system), in order to perform the tasks required to provide the service in that layer. Such communication is termed *peer-to-peer*, as the two tasks have equivalent status within the system.

The peer layers communicate with each other using protocols, a layer's protocol being carried to the peer layer at the other end by the layers below. Each item of information which a layer wishes to send to its peer layer on the remote system is given as a packet to the layer below. The peer-to-peer protocol at each level treats the packet presented to it from above as a stream of data, the structure of which is irrelevant to the current layer. Each layer's protocol will add a header, and sometimes a trailer, to the data passed down from the layer above — a process called *encapsulation*, shown in Fig. 10.3. The headers contain information relevant to that protocol layer,

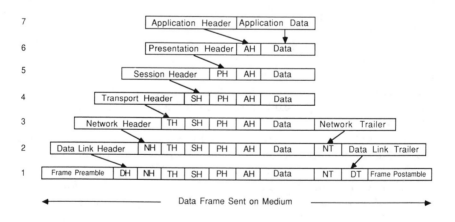

Fig. 10.3 — Example of protocol encapsulation.

and the peer layer on the remote system will strip off its header before passing the remaining packet up to the layer above.

The description of the protocols for each layer forms the second part of the ISO documentation, the *protocol specification*. When ISO protocols are referenced in this book, only the service definition number is given. The corresponding protocol specification can be found in the Appendix. The whole of the ISO model is designed to permit peer-to-peer communications, with each system having the same ability to *initiate* communications. Thus there is no concept of a master/slave relationship between stations, which is common in many proprietary networks.

To return to the ISO model, seven layers or levels are defined for open systems interconnection. As the various services and options have been defined, the figure of seven has tended to be enlarged, through layers sporting sub-layers. Despite defining the model in a top-down manner, the service and protocols have tended to be designed from the middle outwards, as the middle layers were partly in existence, notably the X.25 protocol. The lower layers are now well developed, while much work still remains on the upper layers.

10.3.1   The application layer (layer 7)

Starting at the top of the model, that is, nearest to the user (who is sometimes referred to as 'level 8' of the model!), the *application layer* is by far the most complex. As the development of the standards has progressed from the bottom of the model upwards, it is also the least developed. The main reason for the complexity is the large diversity of applications which may require communications with another system. Although some are fairly obvious, such as the transfer of files between systems, some are not, such as the communications required to operate distributed databases and graphics systems. Provision has also been made at this level for user-written applications, all of which must map onto a common interface to the layer below.

Thus, within the application layer a sub-structure has been defined (DP 7498/4), and a series of documents describing the Common Application Service Elements (CASE, DIS 8649/2&3, DIS 8650/2&3) has been produced. This defines those parts seen to be common to all applications but not included in the lower layers, as they are strictly concerned with applications and not with communications. They can thus be seen as a collection of subroutines available to the application layer entities.

Four main application services have been defined. DP 8831 is concerned with Job Transfer and Manipulation (JTM) — the execution and control on remote systems, of programs resident on one system. DP 8571 describes the procedures for File Transfer, Access and Manipulation (FTAM). Virtual terminal access — interactive access which is not dependent on any specific type of terminal — is covered by several DPs, the basic one being DP 9040. Finally, electronic mail is addressed by a series of documents, the overview being given in DIS 8505, the Message Oriented Text Interchange System (MOTIS).

As an example of a user application, consider a user on one system sending a mail message to a user on another system. The originating user enters his mail message into the MOTIS system on his machine, which imposes some structure on the message, for example the format of the addressee's name and the subject matter or title of the message. Any peer-to-peer interaction between the systems at this level is only to establish parameters relevant to the mail system, such as reporting that a mail message has been read by the recipient.

10.3.2   The presentation layer (layer 6)

The *presentation layer* is concerned with the interpretation of the data, in particular to relieve the applications of concerns about data encryption, page layouts, character codes or graphics conventions. It is this layer which appears to break one of the design aims of the ISO model in that it does not strictly separate the application layer from the session layer (below the presentation layer). Most applications will require direct access to the session layer, and in practice will use the facilities of the presentation layer in much the same way as the Common Application Service Elements mentioned above.

In the electronic mail application example, the presentation layer would translate between machines with incompatible character codes. In theory it is also the layer where a translation between languages, English to Japanese, say, would take place if such a facility were available. As noted above, from this layer downwards, because of the independent layering, the fact that our example is an electronic mail message is not relevant. It can now be considered as a stream of data. The relevant ISO presentation document is DIS 8822.

10.3.3   The session layer (layer 5)

The *session layer* (DIS 8326) is concerned with the management of the dialogue between the two presentation processes. This means controlling the starting, stopping and synchronisation of the conversation. It provides a logical connection, or *session*, between the two systems, which can be full-duplex (data travelling simultaneously in both directions), half-duplex (data travelling first one way, then the other in a coordinated manner), or one way data only.

One of the most significant features of the session layer, which could be used if the message in our example was very large, is *checkpointing*. This involves periodically inserting points into the data from which any recovery necessary can be started. It can thus save retransmitting large quantities of data when connections fail near to the end of a transfer.

10.3.4 The transport layer (layer 4)

The *transport layer* is the last of the layers which are concerned with end-to-end communications, that is, communications between peer entities in the end systems. The transport layer and above are referred to as the upper layers of the model, and they are independent of the underlying network. The lower layers are concerned with data transfer across the network.

The function of the transport layer (DIS 8072) is to provide an *error free* transfer of data between session processes in the end systems. It delivers data in the correct order, without duplication or loss. Depending on the nature of the underlying services, the transport layer offers several different *classes of service,* which may include error recovery and the control of the rate at which data flows between the two processes. The issue of which class to use over a LAN is discussed in the next chapter.

10.3.5   The network layer (layer 3)

The *network layer* is concerned with the transmission of data through a network or series of networks. The important addition at this level is that of the *address* of the machine on which the desired transport entity resides. There has been considerable debate, of particular relevance to LANs, as to what a network is, and the concept of a *subnetwork* is often introduced. Briefly, a subnetwork is a collection of equipment, a LAN for example, whereas a network is the grouping of all connected subnetworks. The network layer is concerned with addressing the entire network, whereas the lower layers address only the subnetwork.

ISO have defined two major services — the connection oriented network service (IS 8348) and its addendum (8348 ADD 1) on connectionless mode services. Again this is of major importance to LANs; further discussion is deferred to the next chapter.

10.3.6   The data link layer (layer 2)

The *data link layer* has the task of preparing the packets passed down from the network layer for transmission on the network. This involves preparing a *frame* of data, which will commonly include checksums for error recovery. As mentioned above, this layer is concerned with transmission on the subnetwork. For example, on a wide area network the data link layer handles transmission to and from the nearest switch. A common example of a data link layer protocol is IBM's HDLC. As described in 10.4, it is at this point that the ISO model starts to break down when applied to LANs.

10.3.7   The physical layer (layer 1)

The *Physical Layer* defines both the electrical and mechanical aspects of the equipment and media involved, and the rules for the transmission of the individual *bits* of the data link layer frame. The former involves the connectors from the station to the cable and the voltage levels to be used in the transmission. The latter includes the type of data encoding, the data rate and the flow control of bits onto and off the medium.

In conclusion, to implement the ISO protocols a *protocol stack* is necessary within each machine (Fig. 10.4). It should be noted that 'conformance to the ISO Model' is a largely meaningless statement, merely stating that 'we too can draw our protocol set as seven layers'. What is important is that each system conforms to the same subset of the ISO protocols.

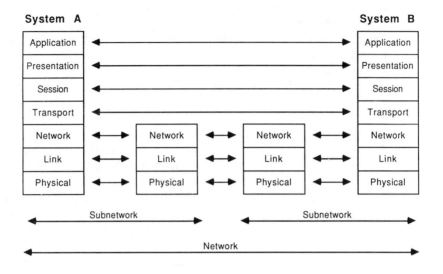

Fig. 10.4 — ISO protocol stacks.

10.4   LANs AND THE ISO OSI REFERENCE MODEL

The ISO Reference Model was designed to enable communication between heterogeneous machines over traditional packet switched networks. When the IEEE started to consider LAN standards they found some problems in fitting LAN requirements to the model. The first problem is that each different physical medium and topology appears to demand a different data link layer, and LANs do not map well onto the point-to-point, i.e. computer to packet switch over a dedicated medium, concepts implied by the model (Fig. 10.4). The solution, a modification of the model, is shown in Fig. 10.5.

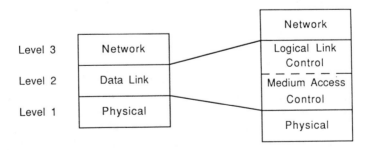

Fig. 10.5 — ISO model as modified for LANs.

The link layer is divided into the *Medium Access Control* (MAC) sublayer, which corresponds to the particular LAN, e.g. CSMA/CD or token ring, and the *Logical Link Control* (LLC) sublayer, which provides the same service to the network layer whichever MAC sublayer is in use. In this way the higher layers can be isolated from the physical LAN details. The LLC also includes provision for *broadcasting*, i.e. sending a packet to all stations on the LAN, which is not covered by the ISO model. The descriptions given in Chapters 7, 8 and 9 were of ISO MAC sublayer protocols.

There are two other major problems for LAN implementors resulting from the OSI reference model. The first is whether a LAN should be considered as a *network* in OSI terms, or as a *subnetwork* which appears as a single *open system* to the wider OSI community. The second is whether *connection oriented* or *connectionless* working is the more appropriate for communications between systems on a LAN. These problems are discussed in the next chapter.

10.5   THE IEEE PROJECT 802 PROTOCOLS

The Institute of Electrical and Electronic Engineers (IEEE), an American professional body. set up Project 802 to define standards for Local Area Networks, and have become the main producer of LAN protocol specifications. To date, four of their standards have been adopted by ISO, namely 802.3 (CSMA/CD), 802.4 (Token Bus), 802.5 (Token Ring) and 802.2 (Logical Link Control).

Project 802, which has restricted itself to the logical link control, MAC and physical layers of the ISO model, is divided into various Working Groups, which produce the standards. Their relationship is shown in Fig. 10.6. In addition, three Technical Advisory Groups (TAGs) advise the

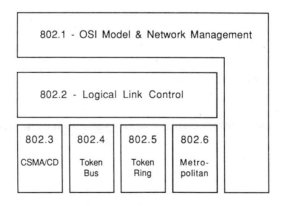

Fig. 10.6 — Organisation of IEEE Project 802.

working groups. The working groups are as follows:

802.1 The High Level Interface group is concerned with the interface between the IEEE standards and the higher layers of the ISO Model.

They are also concerned with network management, e.g. traffic measurement and fault detection, and inter-networking issues.

802.2 The Logical Link Control group is concerned with the services to the network layer. The LLC is common to all the MAC specifications (each of which has its own group) and is discussed further in Chapter 11.

802.3 Carrier Sense Multiple Access/Collision Detection, the Ethernet based access method. This was the subject of Chapter 7.

802.4 Token Bus, which was the subject of Chapter 9.

802.5 Token Ring, which was the subject of Chapter 8.

802.6 Metropolitan Area Networks — city wide networks, which will be compatible with the other LANs, but will also support voice and video traffic. In particular they are examining slotted ring technology based on fibre optics.

802.7 The Broadband Technical Advisory Group is particularly involved with the 802.4 group.

802.8 The Fibre Optic TAG is involved with groups 802.3 and 802.5, although in principle it could apply to all the other groups.

802.9 The most recent TAG is charged with investigating the integration of the LANs with PABX technology.

10.6 STANDARDISATION PROBLEMS

It may appear that the ISO Reference Model, and particularly the IEEE work on LANs and its adherence to the model, has presented the manufacturers with a fixed set of protocols, which when implemented will enable full open systems interworking. There are, however, several reasons why products conforming to the ISO standards have been relatively slow in reaching the marketplace.

First, there is the problem that users are reluctant to buy ISO products until there are a large number of manufacturers who are committed to support them, and the manufacturers are reluctant to develop the products until they are sure of a market. Although there are only seven layers in the ISO model, over 60 ISO standards have now been identified to deal with the many different types of communication, and different manufacturers are choosing to implement different standards at each layer. To quote from a leading networking authority, Tanenbaum (1981): 'The nice thing about standards is that there are so many to choose from'. This is particularly a problem at the LLC and network layers for LANs, and is discussed further in the next chapter. It provides an example of the complexities faced both by the user and the manufacturer at each layer of the model.

In addition to the choice of protocol at each level, within each specification there are usually several classes and, within those, several optional features. Thus the situation can arise that two manufacturers can develop products which are both compatible with the model and the specifications, but which cannot *interwork*. In order for two applications on different systems to communicate, not only do the same protocols have to be implemented at *each* layer, but a common set of classes and options must be selected within each protocol.

This problem is one of the first to be tackled by the increasing number of OSI testing organisations being established in many countries. In the UK, for example, the Department of Trade and Industry has awarded a contract to the Networking Centre to perform some conformance testing, and there is a similar EEC initiative. The work of these centres is twofold: first to establish conformance to the protocol specification, and then to test interworking with other products. It can be expected that they will also give some measure of the operational efficiency of the implementation.

The efficiency of the ISO protocols has been giving rise to some concern, and is often put forward as a good reason for manufacturers not rushing to implement the standards. Recent reports (Strauss 1987) indicate that on 10 Mbit/s networks the best throughput at the transport layer is currently around 1.8 Mbit/s, and that this is limited by the software implementations of the protocols rather than the raw network data rate.

The standards are highly complicated documents, particularly as one goes up the layers, and many years of software and hardware development are needed before an implementation can be released. It has been argued, notably by Padlipsky (1985), that a more efficient path to open systems interconnection would have been to adopt one of the existing, non-manufacturer-specific protocols, such as TCP/IP (Chapter 12).

The advantage of the ISO protocols is the very fact that they have international backing, and most manufacturers have made the commitment to implement them eventually. At present, however, most manufacturers have made their own decisions as to which classes and options to implement at each layer, and despite the user pressure being exerted to coordinate these choices it will be several years before open systems networking becomes a reality. Some of the approaches to achieving this end are examined in Chapter 16.

11

The ISO link layer and above

As noted in the previous chapter, it would require a complete book to give a reasonable overview of all of the ISO protocols. Since they are designed for general *peer-to-peer* communications, however, with only the lowest layers being specifically of interest to LANs, it is reasonable to again refer the reader to Henshall & Shaw (1988) for a description of the transport layers and above.

This chapter describes in some detail the logical link layer, which is specific to LANs, and then discusses the problems for LANs of the network and transport layers, without describing them in detail. The reader is referred to Deasington (1986) for a description of X.25, probably the most famous network layer protocol, and one which forms the basis of one of the ISO network layer protocols.

11.1 THE LOGICAL LINK CONTROL SUB-LAYER

As noted in the previous chapter (Fig. 10.5), the logical link control (LLC) sublayer is that part of the ISO data link layer which is common to, and independent of, all of the different medium access control layers. The first part of this chapter presents a detailed description of the LLC services and protocols, not simply because it is the easiest to grasp, but as it is also illustrative of the approach taken in many of the ISO protocols.

To define any ISO protocol, two documents are produced, a description of the services offered to and by the layer, and a description of the protocol procedures at that layer. In each case, this is further divided into a description of the interface to the lower layer (the MAC layer for LLC), the interface to the higher layer (the network layer for LLC), and a description of the *elements of procedure*, i.e. the details of how the data are transferred between peer entities at that level.

The LLC is concerned with the flow of network layer data between stations *on a single LAN*. It provides the *services* needed to allow the network layer to exchange packets with remote network layer entities, which need *not* be on the same LAN.

Services are provided by one layer for another within an end system (a system at one end of the conversation) by the interchange of *primitives*, i.e. messages, of which there are three basic types. All the ISO protocols are defined in terms of these generic types:

REQUEST   by which the user of a service requests that a service be initiated.

INDICATION   by which the provider of the service indicates to the user that an event has occurred, for example that an incoming packet has arrived.

CONFIRM   by which the service provider indicates completion of a previously requested service.

No ISO specification defines or implies any specific implementation details. For example, the method by which the primitives are passed between layers, whether each layer is a separate process in a machine, how the data are buffered — these are not defined but are left entirely to the implementor. The only important point is that the external view of an implementation must conform to the specification.

11.2   THE MAC LAYER SERVICE INTERFACE

The interface between the MAC sub-layer and the LLC sub-layer is one of the simplest possible in ISO terms, comprising only three primitives, as shown in Fig. 11.1. (Note that the same three MAC primitives shown in Fig

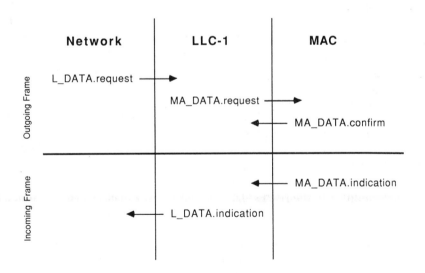

Fig. 11.1 — LLC Type 1 service primitives.

11.1 apply to all the LLC types). Using the ISO jargon, they are:

MA_DATA.request   Requests the MAC layer to send an LLC packet to a specified address.

MA_DATA.indication	Comes from the MAC layer to inform the LLC that a packet has arrived addressed to it.
MA_DATA.confirm	Tells the LLC that the packet it has requested to be sent has been sent, or has failed to be sent. Note that this *does not imply receipt by the other end*, only that the frame was transmitted onto the medium.

11.3   THE NETWORK LAYER SERVICE INTERFACE

As noted earlier, for two systems to interwork the same protocols and options must be chosen at each layer of the ISO model. The first of the many protocol choices presents itself at the LLC sublayer, in that there are three *classes of service* defined, using three *types* of operation.

The *UNACKNOWLEDGED CONNECTIONLESS* service, known as LLC-1, uses Type 1 operations, and enables network layer entities to exchange data without the establishment of a link level connection, or virtual circuit, i.e. it uses datagrams. Since the MAC level frames are essentially datagram in nature, this maps particularly well onto LAN architectures. In this very simple class of service there is no guaranteed delivery, nor is any indication of success or failure indicated to the network layer, i.e. there is no 'confirm' primitive.

The second type of service is termed *CONNECTION ORIENTED*, and the LLC-2 class of services consists of this type plus Type 1. Type 2 operation requires the establishment of a *connection*, i.e. a virtual circuit, between the two LLC entities in the communicating stations, along which the data units are passed. Note that although there will generally only be two stations involved, the protocol allows for multicast and broadcast transmission. Type 2 operation provides for the correct sequencing of the data, guarantees delivery by including error recovery, and offers control of the flow of data. It is very close to, and is based upon, the X.25 LAPB link level protocol, commonly used in wide area networks.

The third service class is termed *ACKNOWLEDGED CONNECTION-LESS*, LLC-3. This uses Type 3 procedures, which are essentially LLC-1 with the addition of acknowledged receipt of packets. It has been a late addition to the IEEE 802.2 specifications, and has still to be ratified by ISO. For the purpose of clarity, and since this chapter's aim is to illustrate rather than be a definitive guide to the protocols, only Type 1 and Type 2 procedures will be described; Type 3 is restricted in practice to the process control type of environment, particularly on token bus LANs.

11.3.1   The unacknowledged connectionless service

There are only two primitives defined between the network and the LLC layers for the Type 1 operation, namely:

L_DATA.request	by which the network layer requests that the LLC layer transmits a packet.

L_DATA.indication   by which the LLC layer indicates to the network
                                 layer that a packet has arrived for it.

Fig. 11.1 illustrates how the primitives are used. Note that although the
MAC layer indicates the success or failure of the transmission to the LLC
layer, this is not passed on to the network layer. There is also an implied
relative time of events in Fig. 11.1, from the top down. This is a typical
example of the time sequence diagrams used in the specifications themselves
to clarify valid sequences of events.

11.3.2   The connection oriented service

The Type 2 operation is somewhat more complex, and can be split into three
phases, connection establishment, data transfer, and connection termina-
tion. There are also some primitives for error recovery and for controlling
the flow of data.

The service primitives for all three phases are shown in Fig. 11.2, along

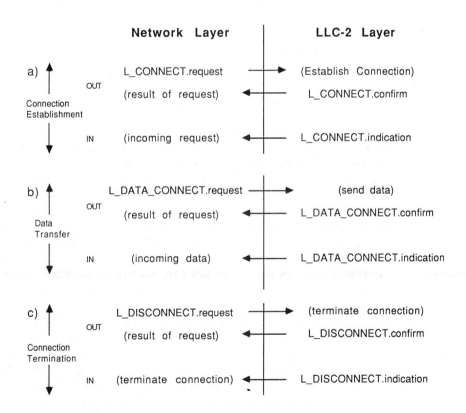

Fig. 11.2 — LLC Type 2 service primitives.

with their meaning. In addition the L_RESET primitives (request, indication and confirm) are used to reset the link back to its initial state, as if it had just been established. This is used in error recovery situations when it is not desirable to drop the link and re-establish it again. The final two primitives are L_CONNECT_FLOWCONTROL request and indication, which can enable the network layer to restrict the flow of data along the LLC connection.

11.4   LLC PROTOCOL DATA UNIT STRUCTURE AND PROCEDURES

Chapter 10 described the process of *encapsulation*, whereby each layer appends its own header to the data passed down to it from the layer above. This header, plus the encapsulated data, is called a Protocol Data Unit (PDU), and its format for LLC is shown in Fig. 11.3.

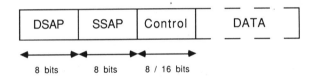

Fig. 11.3 — Logical link control PDU format.

A service at any layer of the ISO model must have an *address*, i.e. a unique identifier within the station by which remote stations can access it. These addresses are termed *service access points*, usually prefixed by the letter describing the layer. Thus the LLC service access points, which are network layer service addresses, are known as LSAPs. By this mechanism, multiple services can be offered at each layer. Note that the SAPs are also conceptually the access points for the higher layer to address the lower layer.

As Fig. 11.3 shows, the LSAPs are eight bits long, and each LLC packet carries both the source and the destination LSAPs, known as the SSAP and the DSAP respectively. Thus each LLC packet on the LAN carries the identifier of the network layer service which sent the packet, and the identifier of the network layer service which is the intended recipient. The LLC layer can then route the encapsulated network layer packet to the correct network service. The values of the LSAPs are globally allocated for the different services by the IEEE, and the top bit of each has special significance. In the DSAP, the setting of the top bit implies that this is a multicast address (cf. MAC frame descriptions in Chapters 7, 8 and 9), with 'all 1s' indicating the broadcast LLC address. The top bit of the SSAP is used to indicate whether the PDU contains a command, or a response to a command, the significance of which is described below.

The control field of the PDU is either 8 or 16 bits long, depending on the type of PDU. There are three types of PDU, each of which has a number of commands and responses to those commands. The format of the control field for each of the types is shown in Fig. 11.4. Note that the information

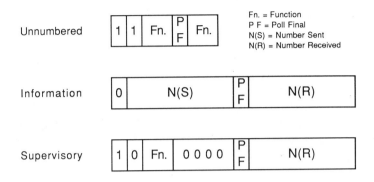

Fig. 11.4 — Format of control field of LLC PDU.

and supervisory types are only used by the Type 2 protocol, whereas both Type 2 and Type 1 use the unnumbered commands. The following description of the commands illustrates the procedures of the protocol.

11.4.1 Unnumbered format commands

There are five unnumbered format commands, and five responses. They are:

UI   *Unnumbered information*, which is the command used by Type 1 to send data frames. This is the only unnumbered command which carries data.

XID   *Exchange identification*, which is both a command and a response to the command. It is used by both Type 1 and Type 2 as an 'are you still there?' message, and by Type 2 to establish and adjust the window size (see 11.4.2 below).

TEST   The *Test* command is both a command and a response to the command. It is used to perform a basic loopback test over the LLC transmission path.

FRMR   *Frame reject* is a response which covers protocol violations, i.e. unexpected events, such as out of sequence frames.

   The remaining Unnumbered Format commands are used to establish and disconnect connections within Type 2 operation.

SABME   *Set asynchronous balanced mode extended*, requests the establishment of a connection. The title distinguishes it from other types of connection used in other protocols.

UA   *Unnumbered acknowledgment* is the response to a SABME when the receiver is accepting the call.

DM   *Disconnect mode* is the response to a SABME when the receiver does not wish to accept the call.

DISC   *Disconnect* is the command sent when one station wishes to close the connection. It is acknowledged by either a UA or a DM response, both of which indicate that the call is now closed.

11.4.2 Information transfer command

In Type 2 operation there is only one command and response packet for information transfer, i.e. the packets in which the network layer data is sent over the connection. This is known as the *I frame* (Information) and its control field format is shown in Fig. 11.4. When the connection is established, both stations set two counts — N(S) 'S' for send, and N(R) 'R' for receive — to zero. Separate counts are maintained for each connection which is established. Every time an LLC sends an information packet it increments the N(S) count, and every time an information packet is correctly received N(R) is incremented. Thus each LLC keeps track of the packets flowing in each direction. When the count reaches the value 127, it returns to zero, i.e. it is modulo 128.

The N(S) count in the control field gives the packet its reference number, and thus lets the receiver determine if the packets are arriving in the correct order. The N(R) count is used by the receiver to indicate to the sender the frame number which it next expects to receive, which implies that it has received all the frames up to and including the one numbered N(R)-1. The sender is permitted to send up to a set maximum number of frames before it must wait for an acknowledgment from the receiver. This number is determined at the start of the connection, using the XID frame, and is known as the *window size*.

The windowing technique is commonly used on connection based protocols as it is very efficient, although it can mean the retransmission of many frames if one is corrupt. Furthermore the sender must keep a copy of all of the packets sent until an acknowledgment is received. The use of N(R) in an information packet is an efficient way of acknowledging receipt of packets when data is flowing in both directions. When data is only flowing in one direction, the supervisory commands must be used.

The final part of the control field is the P/F bit, which stands for Poll/Final, and this provides another 'are you there?' sequence which is used under certain error conditions.

11.4.3 Supervisory format commands

Fig. 11.4 also shows the format of the control field for supervisory format commands, which are only used in Type 2 operation. The P/F and N(R) fields have the same significance as in the information transfer commands. There are three supervisory format packets, each of which can be a command or a response.

RR   *Receiver ready* indicates that the receiver is ready to receive another frame. It is used to acknowledge frames when no data frames are available. When the link is idle, RR frames are sent every few seconds to keep the link alive.

RNR   *Receiver not ready* indicates a temporary busy condition at the receiver. The sender should not transmit any more packets until another RR is received.

REJ   *Frame reject* is used to request the transmission of all the frames after and including the frame number in N(R). This is used to recover from frames arriving out of sequence.

A simplified example of an error-free Type 2 conversation is shown in Fig. 11.5.

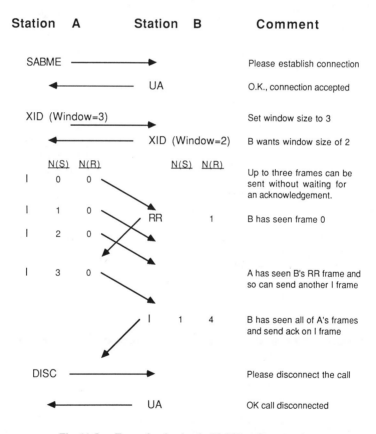

Fig. 11.5 — Example of a simple LLC Type 2 connection.

It can be seen from the above simplified description of the logical link layer, one of the most straightforward ISO protocols, that the implementation and conformance testing of all the protocols at all of the layers is a non-trivial exercise.

11.5   THE NETWORK AND TRANSPORT LAYERS

The LAN system implementor — the person selecting the software to run over the LAN — is presented with further choices at the ISO network layer, which in turn influence the choice to be made at the transport layer.

There are two services defined for the network layer (IS 8348), the *Connection Oriented Network Service* (CONS) and the *ConnectionLess Network Service* (CLNS). Similarly, at the transport layer (IS 8072), there are the *Connection Mode Service* and the *Connectionless Service*. Both of the connectionless services were late addenda to the original service definition. The connection mode transport service is complicated further by offering five classes of service, 0 to 4, ranging from the very simple classes (0–2), which can be used when the underlying network layer protocol offers full facilities, to the very complex class (4), which is for use when the underlying network service performs a basic service only.

Thus the logical expectation would be to use one of the stack of protocols shown in Fig 11.6, depending on whether a connection oriented or a

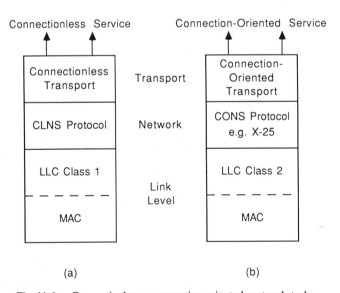

Fig. 11.6 — Connectionless v. connection-oriented protocol stacks.

connectionless service were being offered at the transport level. LANs, however, have traditionally been regarded as connectionless, because of the datagram nature of the MAC layer. The original uses of LANs, to support high speed connection for extracting pages from a file store, have also been oriented towards connectionless applications, and thus would benefit from the connectionless stack shown in Fig. 11.6.

For open systems working, however, most of the current applications, for example a remote terminal session or file transfer, are highly connection oriented, and thus require the connection service at the transport level. If one tries to preserve the simplicity of LLC-1 and the simple CLNS network layer, this implies the implementation of the full Class 4 transport layer, which merely pushes the complexity of the network layer one stage up in the model (Fig. 11.7(a)). This has been taken further in some implementations in the situation where a single LAN can be considered to be the whole network. In this case it can be argued that the LLC and MAC layers provide all the necessary functionality of the network layer, in that every station can be addressed, and thus no network layer is required at all (Fig. 11.7(b)).

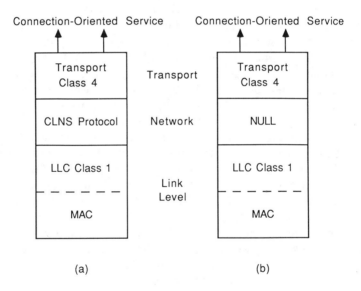

Fig. 11.7 — Connection-oriented transport service over LLC class 1.

In the future, however, it is unlikely that LANs will exist in isolation — they will require to be linked to wide area networks. Connection to a wide area network is done through a station called a *gateway*, whose function will be examined again in Chapter 16. A gateway allows stations on the LAN to communicate with stations on the WAN, or with stations on another LAN which is also connected to the WAN. In OSI terms, it does not matter how many, or of what nature, the subnetworks are. The gateway must match the protocols used on the LAN with those used on the WAN, and it is part of the ISO network layer definitions that this should be done only at the network layer and below.

Thus a gateway can be pictured as in Fig. 11.8, picking up LLC and network layer packets on either side, and translating them into whatever is required on the other side. The transport layer is thus preserved as the 'end-process to end-process' protocol, with no need to concern itself about the route, as per the ISO Model definition. Since almost all wide area networks are connection oriented, with X.25 being well established and now expanded to provide the ISO Connection Oriented Network Service, it can be expected that most gateways will have to map to a connection service on the WAN. This is obviously much easier if the same CONS service is being offered on the LAN. In practice the connection oriented protocol for the network layer on the LAN is an extension of X.25. (It has to be an extension as X.25 assumes DTE to DCE working, i.e. from a station to a packet switch. On a LAN the network entities have to determine which will be the DTE and which the DCE).

There is much resistance to the idea of running protocols such as LLC-2 and Connection Oriented Network, which were originally designed to run over slow error-prone networks, on fast error-free networks. An argument is thus presented that every station on a LAN need not be considered to be an Open System, but that the whole LAN should present itself to the WAN as a single Open System (Burg and Chen 1984). In this case, the LAN as a whole should not be considered as part of the network in ISO terms. ISO regard a network as a collection of systems who are able to communicate with each other, and so to try to prevent confusion, a LAN connected to a wide area network in this way is termed a *sub-network*.

There are several arguments against this approach, however, the first being that some stations on the LAN would undoubtedly wish to be seen as Open Systems. It has been estimated that up to 30% of the LAN traffic could be targeted to the WAN, and this would put a very high load on a very complex gateway (Burg & Chen 1984). Secondly, although the transmission medium is virtually error free, the speeds of LANs place a great strain on the end systems, and many LLC frames are lost because the receiving station cannot keep up with the network. This is especially true of, say, a front end to a mainframe, which may be dealing with many stations simultaneously, and therefore may wish to run the connection oriented protocols to gain the flow control features. This is also the argument against running the connection oriented network protocol over LLC-1. Because of the layer independence of the ISO model, this is perfectly possible, but the lack of control in LLC-1 can cause problems at the network layer.

ISO DIS 8880 (Protocol Combinations to Provide and Support the Network Service) attempts to clarify the situation by specifying different environments within which a network service will be required. Within each environment, one of which is LANs, valid combinations of protocols are defined such that any system claiming conformance to the ISO specification must support those combinations. It states that such systems on a LAN would have to support LLC-2, the connection oriented protocol at the network layer (CONS), and transport Class 2, *for those applications which are connection oriented*. Recently, however, this has been relaxed to permit

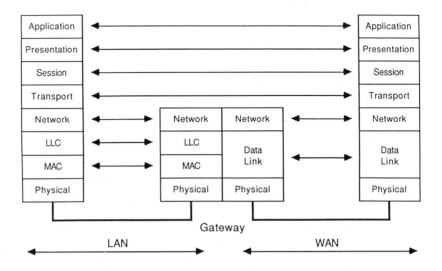

Fig. 11.8 — LAN to WAN gateway functions.

LLC-1 to be used. The situation therefore remains confused, but one possible solution is the definition of *functional standards*, which are the subject of Chapter 16.

12

Non-ISO protocols

Although it is the ISO open systems protocols which have received most recent publicity, there are other well established protocol sets, particularly on Ethernet, which have a large share of the current LAN market. Some, notably Padlipsky (1985), argue that these protocols offer a better alternative to the largely untried and potentially cumbersome ISO set, but most manufacturers indicate a willingness to adopt ISO protocols at some point in the future.

The two non-ISO protocols described in this chapter illustrate two different approaches from the ISO protocol set to Open Systems working. The first, TCP/IP, is a vendor-independent wide area network protocol set, which been widely used on LANs for peer-to-peer communications. The second is SUN Microsystem's NFS, which is targeted at workstation-to-filestore access. It provides a contrast to the ISO style and a link to the PC protocols discussed in the next chapter.

12.1 TCP/IP

The suite of protocols commonly referred to as TCP/IP, which stands for *Transmission Control Protocol / Internet Protocol* (US Military Standards 1778 and 1777), was developed by the United States Department of Defense for its A.R.P.A. (Advanced Research Project Agency) network. This is a very large scale, wide area, network linking many major commercial, university and military establishments. The relevance of TCP/IP to LANs is twofold. First, as it is a datagram based protocol, it is well suited to LAN access methods, particularly Ethernet. Secondly, it is particularly popular within the UNIX community, giving it a large user base, many of whom wish to use LANs.

The structure of the TCP/IP protocol set is shown in Fig. 12.1, along with the approximately equivalent ISO model layers. Network file system is included for completeness; it is examined in 12.2. It can be seen that this is essentially a five layer model, although the layers are not as clear cut as in the ISO model, and the model has been drawn from analysis of what is used, rather than being defined first and then the protocols specified. The TCP/IP philosophy, described in detail in Padlipsky (1985), is the antithesis of the ISO philosophy. In ISO protocols, everything appears to be put into the

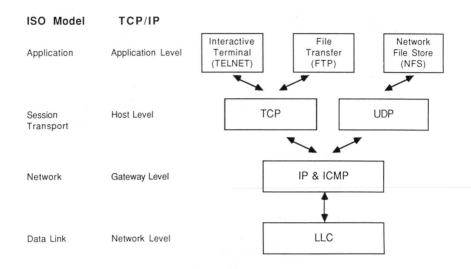

ISO Model   TCP/IP

Fig. 12.1 — TCP/IP protocol relationships.

protocol, but parts are made optional. In TCP/IP, the protocols are kept very simple. If more functionality is required, then another protocol is added to deal with the situation. The main protocols are as follows:

IP   The *Internet Protocol*, which provides a connectionless data-gram 'network' layer.

ICMP   The *Internet Control Message Protocol*, is an example of the bolt-on approach mentioned above. It adds functionality to the IP protocol and can be considered as an extension to that protocol.

UDP   The *User Datagram Protocol* provides the rough equivalent of the ISO connectionless transport service.

TCP   The *Transmission Control Protocol* is a connection oriented, reliable, end-to-end transport protocol.

The protocols which run above TCP include *TELNET*, a terminal access protocol, and a file transfer protocol *FTP*. The four main protocols are now examined further as a contrast to the ISO approach.

12.1.1 The internet protocol (IP)

There is a second difference in philosophy between ISO and the TCP/IP approach, which revolves around the word 'network'. In the TCP/IP model, a network is an individual packet switched network which may be a LAN or a WAN, but is generally under the control of one organisation. These networks connect to each other by gateways, and the resulting collection of such networks is called a *catenet* (from concatenation). The internet protocol provides for the transmission of datagrams between systems over the whole catenet. It specifically allows for the fragmentation and re-assembly of the datagrams at the gateways, as the underlying networks may demand different packet sizes.

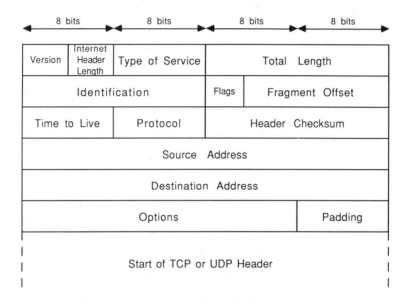

Fig. 12.2 — Format of an internet datagram header.

The *Internet Protocol* (US Military Standard 1771) is a very simple protocol, with no mechanisms for end-to-end data reliability, flow control or sequencing. The header, however, shown in Fig. 12.2, is quite complex, the fields being as follows:

Version
: The version number of IP. There have been several new releases, which (given the size of ARPANET) must co-exist for some time.

IHL
: The IP header length. Because of the options field, the header is not a fixed length. This field shows where the data starts.

Type of service
: This field allows for a priority system to be imposed, plus an indication of the desired, but not guaranteed, reliability required.

Length
: The total length of the IP packet. Although there is a theoretical maximum of 64 Kbytes, most networks operate with much smaller packets, though all must accept at least 576 bytes.

ID/flags/offset
: These fields enable a gateway to split up the datagram into smaller segments. The ID field

	ensures that the receiver can piece together the fragments from the correct datagram, as fragments from many datagrams may arrive in any order. The offset tells how far down the datagram this fragment is, and the flags can be used to mark the datagram as non-fragmentable.
Time to live	This is a count which limits the lifetime of a datagram on the catenet. Each time it passes through a gateway, the count is decremented by one. If it reaches zero, the gateway does not forward it. This prevents permanently circulating datagrams.
Protocol	This indicates which higher level protocol is being carried, e.g. TCP or UDP.
Checksum	This checksum covers the header only. It is up to the higher layers to detect transmission errors in the data.
Source/dest address	To assist the gateways to route datagrams by the most efficient path, each IP address is structured into a Network Number and a local address. There are three classes of network, providing different numbers of locally administered addresses.
Options	The final part of the header is a variable number of optional fields, which are used to enforce security or network management.
Padding	This field is used to align the header to the next 32-bit boundary.

Because there is no facility for error reporting in IP, for example the sender of a datagram is not informed if the intended recipient is available, an extra protocol is used, particularly to help gateways between networks. This is called the *Internet Control Message Protocol* (ICMP) which, although it is carried over IP, is considered to be an integral part of it. It does not help in making IP reliable, however, it merely reports errors without trying to recover from them.

Examples of ICMP messages include *TIME EXCEEDED* when the lifetime of a datagram expires, and *DESTINATION UNREACHABLE* when a gateway or network has failed. The gateways also exchange routing information using another extra protocol, called the *gateway-to-gateway* protocol. This enables the gateways to have up-to-date information on the loading on certain routes, so that bottlenecks can be avoided.

12.1.2 User datagram protocol (UDP)

The *User Datagram Protocol* (UDP) provides a connectionless transport service to applications. Unlike the ISO protocols, which are layer independent, it assumes that IP is running below, and implementations must have access to incoming IP headers.

The UDP header, shown in Fig. 12.3, is very simple, and can be considered as an extension of the IP header to permit multiple services to be addressed within the same IP network address.

12.1.3 Transmission control protocol

The *Transmission Control Protocol* (TCP) (US Military Standard 1781) provides a highly reliable, connection oriented, end-to-end transport service between processes in end systems connected to the catenet. TCP only assumes that the layer below offers an unreliable datagram service, and thus could run over any such protocols. In practice, however, it is invariably linked to IP. TCP provides the types of facility associated with the ISO Class 4 transport service, including error recovery, sequencing of packets, flow control by the windowing method, and the support of multiplexed connections from the layer above. The format of the TCP header is shown in Fig. 12.4. The operational procedures are similar to the ISO connection oriented protocols, such as LLC Type 2 (compare with Chapter 11). The fields in the header are as follows:

Source/dest ports	These fields identify multiple streams to the layer above.
Sequence/ack number	These are used for the windowing acknowledgment technique described in Chapter 11.
Data Offset	This is the number of 32-bit words in the TCP header which, like the IP header, has a variable length options field.
Flag bits	There are several bits used as status indicators to show, for example, the resetting of the connection.
Window	This field is used by the receiver to set the window size.
Checksum	Again this covers only the header.
Urgent pointer	The sender can indicate that an urgent datagram is coming and urges the receiver to handle it as quickly as possible.
Options	This variable-sized field contains some negotiation parameters, to set the size of the TCP packets for example.
Padding	To align to the next 32-bit boundary.

The procedures used by the TCP protocol are too complex to describe here. It can be seen, however, that the catenet style of networking has benefits for linking LANs — hence the widespread use of TCP/IP on LANs. It should not be assumed, however, that TCP/IP networks are immune from the compatibility problems discussed earlier for ISO networks. Differences in interpretation of the protocols can drastically reduce interoperability and there are reports of deficiencies in many of the protocols (Borsook 1987). One interesting recent development, however, is an experimental implementation of the ISO transport service on top of TCP, which means that ISO

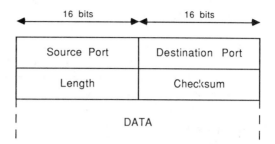

Fig. 12.3 — Format of user datagram protocol header.

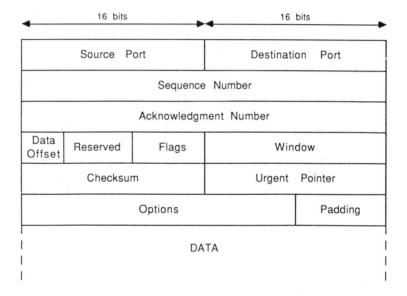

Fig. 12.4 — Format of TCP header.

applications could be carried over IP catenets (Rose & Cass 1987). TCP/IP can also co-exist with ISO and other protocols on a LAN, and it can be expected that the production of protocol converters should ease the transition between TCP/IP and ISO for many users.

12.2   NETWORK FILE SYSTEM

SUN Microsystem's *Network File System* (NFS) is an interesting example of a protocol designed for remote file access from workstations to a file server over a LAN. Although mainly implemented under the UNIX operating system, principally SUN's own range of workstations, the protocol itself is both machine and operating system independent.

One of the main aims of NFS is to present the remote files to a program running on a workstation as if they were local to that workstation. Thus a program does not need to know the location of the file. In the UNIX environment, files are organised into an hierarchical tree structure, with each user having his or her own tree, under the user's name. The remote file system is perceived as being an extra set of branches to the tree, with each user having a specific hierarchy of directories on the remote file server. Each system has a directory '/usr', in which the users' names appear, and the remote file system is seen as a subdirectory (another user), '/usr/src', as shown in Fig. 12.5.

12.2.1   RPC and XDR

The network filestore system achieves its machine and operating system independence in two ways. First it is implemented by means of a *Remote Procedure Call* (RPC) mechanism. Like the procedure or subroutine methods adopted in programs, RPCs help to clarify the structure of the protocol implementation, which is defined in terms of procedure calls with parameters being passed and results returned.

A further similarity with program subroutines is that control is not returned to the calling process until the RPC has completed and the result known. For example, to create a new file on the file server, the NFS protocol handler calls the *CREATE* procedure, whose parameters include the directory, name and attributes of the file being created (Fig. 12.6). The underlying transport mechanism passes this information to the file server over the LAN, the file is created, and a response indicating the success or failure of the action, plus a reference for future accesses to that file, is returned. Only at that point is control returned to the NFS protocol handler.

The second facility for achieving system independence is that the protocols are described using an *eXternal Data Representation* package, called XDR. XDR defines the byte ordering, alignment and size of the main types of data, for example strings, integers and arrays. This makes it possible for implementors to produce new NFS systems without having to reconstruct their own system's internal data representation formats to suit NFS.

One major difference between NFS and the ISO style of protocols is that the NFS protocol is *stateless*. All of the information necessary to complete a procedure call is contained within the parameters to that call, and in particular the server does not keep track of any previous calls. (In a protocol such as LLC Type 2, described in Chapter 11, both stations involved in the call must remember the state that the call is in, for example whether a response is expected from the other end and what the next sequence number is. Such protocols are driven by state tables, large matrices of what the protocol handler should do next for any given event happening in any given state, for example a reset arriving when a machine has just sent out a disconnect request.)

A large part of the ISO specifications is taken up with these state tables,

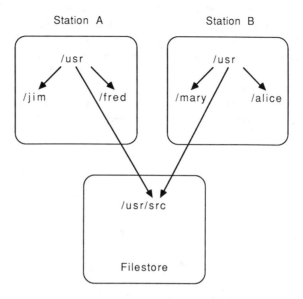

Fig. 12.5 — Example of NFS UNIX file directory extensions

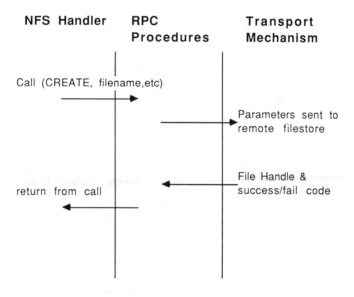

Fig. 12.6 — Example of remote procedure call interface.

but one of the great difficulties with state driven protocols is dealing with the problems of one system crashing in mid-conversation. It is usually necessary for each system to be able to detect that the other has crashed and tidy up accordingly. The great advantage of the NFS stateless approach is that error recovery is simple. If a client station crashes, then the server will not know and has no action to take. When a server crashes, then any client will simply keep sending requests until it gets a response. It is impossible to lose data when a server crashes as it only sends responses back to requests when the action has completed.

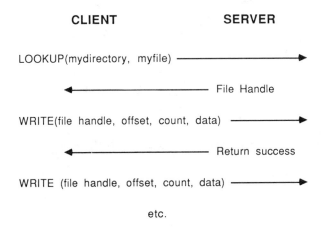

CLIENT   **SERVER**

LOOKUP(mydirectory, myfile) ─────────────────▶

◀───────────────── File Handle

WRITE(file handle, offset, count, data) ─────────▶

◀───────────────── Return success

WRITE (file handle, offset, count, data) ─────────▶

etc.

Fig. 12.7 — Example of a stateless file access.

Fig. 12.7 illustrates a typical sequence of events, in this case writing to a file which already exists. It is assumed that the user on the client workstation has access permission to write to the file. The client must first find a *file handle* (a short reference identifier) for the file, which it then uses in subsequent calls. This is done by calling the LOOKUP procedure, with the full directory and name of the file. The file server will ensure that the file exists, then passes back the file handle. Writing data to the file is simply a matter of calling the WRITE procedure. This has four parameters, namely the file handle, the offset down the file at which the data is to start, a count of the number of bytes of the data, and the data itself. The server will only return a response when it is certain that the data has been written to permanent storage.

Note that there is no concept of opening or closing a file, as this would be state dependent, and thus any client can read or write arbitrary parts of any file for which the file handle was known. This process is very efficient, but introduces a major drawback, in that two clients can write to the same area of the same file, and what ends up in the file depends on who writes last. This problem is overcome by the implementation of a file locking protocol, in addition to NFS. The remaining procedures in NFS are concerned with the creation of directories, the deletion of files and directories, and the gathering of statistics, in much the same way as a local disc would be handled.

Although it could be implemented over any transport service, NFS only requires an unreliable service, and on most systems it is implemented over the User Datagram Protocol described earlier in the chapter. Even if packets get lost on the network, the stateless nature of NFS implies easy recovery, and NFS over UDP leads to very efficient remote file access. The remote accessing of files from workstations was one of the earliest problems to be addressed, as LANs were originally intended to support this style of operation. This has also occupied the manufacturers of Personal Computers, which is the subject of the next chapter.

13

Personal computer networking standards

The previous two chapters have described protocols specifically developed for general peer-to-peer communications between different machines running different operating systems. For PC systems, however (this chapter restricts itself to the IBM PC and its clones) there has been no such standardisation effort, and the market has developed largely by adopting de facto standards.

To date, there have been three major developments relevant to LANs centred on the IBM PC. The first was IBM's production of the NETBIOS interface, which has freed software developers from concerning themselves with the details of the network hardware. The second was the extensions to Microsoft's MS-DOS, from version 3.1 onwards, which enabled a PC to provide primitives for a multi-access file service. Finally, building on the first two developments have come a series of Network Operating Systems (NOS), which provide an integrated package for the end user.

13.1 NETBIOS

IBM's *NETwork Basic Input/Output System*, (NETBIOS), was announced in mid-1984, and was the first step in the rationalisation of PC networking software (Stieglitz 1985). IBM have freely published the details of the NETBIOS interface, and have thus encouraged other manufacturers to produce NETBIOS emulations. As it is IBM's intention to support the NETBIOS interface on future LANs and PCs — indeed it has been carried forward to IBM's new Personal System/2 range — most PC LAN manufacturers have designed software to comply with the interface. The most interesting facet of NETBIOS is that it was an attempt to break away from the centralised disc server-controlled PC network, in that it supports PC-to-PC communication without any intermediate machine being involved in the transaction.

NETBIOS presents a fixed interface between the PC's operating system and the LAN, independent of the LAN hardware or software. In concept, NETBIOS is similar to IBM's earlier BIOS (Basic Input/Output System), which provides an interface between the operating system and the hardware components (discs, printers, etc.) of the PC. In the same way that the BIOS (correctly used) freed the programmer from having to implement several different versions of a program to reflect the differences in the underlying hardware, so the NETBIOS frees the programmer from the same task for each different LAN.

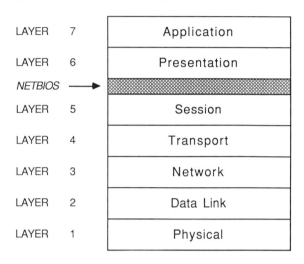

Fig. 13.1 — Position of NETBIOS interface relative to ISO model.

In terms of the ISO reference model, the NETBIOS is an interface between the session layer and the presentation layer as shown in Fig. 13.1, and is thus a peer-to-peer interface. It supports both virtual circuit and datagram services, and it includes a mechanism for mapping station name to network address. In theory, therefore, any protocols at the transport layer and below could be run under NETBIOS, although most of the Network Operating Systems use their own proprietary protocols above the LLC layer. It is quite conceivable, however, that future PCs could run the full ISO set of protocols under the NETBIOS interface, perhaps during a transition phase before full ISO implementation.

On many hardware implementations, the NETBIOS support is provided in read-only memory (ROM) on the LAN interface card. This is the case, for example, in IBM's PC-Network and token ring (Fig. 13.7). If the interface card has its own microprocessor, this obviously relieves the PC's own processor from a great deal of processing. The interface to the operating system is implemented by calling functions in the standard manner, i.e. via a software interrupt. A degree of operating system independence is maintained by passing only a pointer to a *Network Control Block (NCB)*, the format of which is shown in Fig. 13.2.

The NCB is used to pass information in both directions across the NETBIOS interface, the COMMAND being passed from the caller to NETBIOS, and the RETURN CODE from NETBIOS back to the caller. A

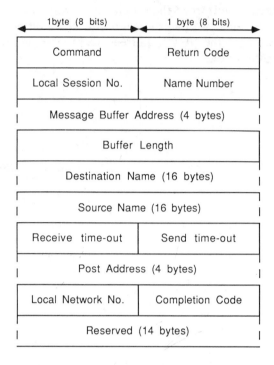

Fig. 13.2 — Format of NETBIOS network control block.

process making a NETBIOS call must set up the NCB in its memory area, call NETBIOS, then wait for NETBIOS to return. There is also a 'no wait' option, whereby control is returned immediately to the process, NETBIOS interrupting the process at the POST ADDRESS given in the NCB when the task is complete.

The other parameters in the NCB are largely concerned with session management. Any single PC has a unique station name, usually held in ROM on the interface board, and can also have up to 16 user defined process names associated with it. It is these process names which are used to set up calls. This has the advantage of not tying a process to a given machine. If, for example, the accounts department have a printer spooler process running on one machine, which then develops a fault, it can simply be started up on another machine without re-configuring the network. In addition, a process name can have more than one session associated with it, with up to 32 simultaneous sessions being supported by NETBIOS.

The actual session commands supported include what one might expect, namely *CALL* to open a session, *LISTEN* for a call, *SEND* and *RECEIVE*, plus *HANGUP* to close the call. There are also separate DATAGRAM commands and several management commands, for example for adding names to the system and removing names. An interesting side effect of the naming scheme is that when a new name is added, the station polls (or broadcasts a request if the LAN permits) to all the other PCs on the LAN to make sure that the name is unique. A similar technique is used to find the name required when a session call is made: the calling station broadcasts to all the stations on the LAN to find out which station name currently owns the requested process.

Although the naming system is very flexible, and has the great attraction of user defined names, it is also one of NETBIOS's major deficiencies. On a very large LAN and particularly on a network consisting of many interlinked LANs, it could take a long time to find out the station address of a given named process. This is one of the areas addressed by several of the Network Operating Systems.

13.2   MS-DOS 3.1

While NETBIOS provides PC-to-PC communication, the main PC operating systems in existence when it was first released provided no facilities for remote access to resources over a network. It was not until the release of Microsoft's MS-DOS 3.1 in late 1984 that the concept of accessing files at a remote file server, simultaneously with other users, became a possibility (Hurwitz 1985). Before then, some file server LANs were in existence, but each had its own rules for file access and particularly for file locking, and thus there was a serious disincentive for any applications programmer to develop a network wide applications program, as a different version would have had to be maintained for every file server system.

Of the extensions added to the existing DOS (Disc Operating System), the most crucial was a new file access mode, called *shared*, which permits a file to be accessed simultaneously by more than one program. This is a prerequisite for any networked application, a shared database for example. Several other additions were required. The first was *byte locking*, whereby one program can lock others out from a specified range of bytes within a file while they are being updated. The second was the extended use of *file handles* (which were introduced in an earlier version of DOS) in a manner very similar to that of the Network File System, described in the previous chapter.

Another problem which the new MS-DOS addressed was the use of temporary files by an application. If a multi-user application opens a temporary file, the system must ensure that separate temporary files are maintained for each user. MS-DOS has a new call, *CREATE TEMPORARY FILE*, which allocates a unique file name, rather than the old method of the application requesting a specifically named file to be opened. New permanent files are opened in a similar manner. The file handle method is an addition to the existing single user File Control Block system, which is similar in concept to the NCBs mentioned earlier. However, MS-DOS 3.1 still provides the usual operating system services to applications programs resident locally, in terms of access to the terminal and other peripherals.

The final crucial addition by Microsoft was an application program, the *Redirector*. The Redirector redirects calls from the local disc to a remote file service. It is the Redirector which makes the difference between a *disc server* and a *file server*. Many early LANs were based on disc servers, where each client saw the shared disc as an extension of its own disc space, unaware of the other clients, and sent ordinary disc commands, for example to read specific physical disc blocks. A file server system imposes a disc accessing protocol between the server and the client. Thus the client talks to the Redirector, which passes requests to the file server, which returns a result. Like the NFS system this is much easier to handle for networked applications, and it removes from the application the need for any knowledge of the physical disc.

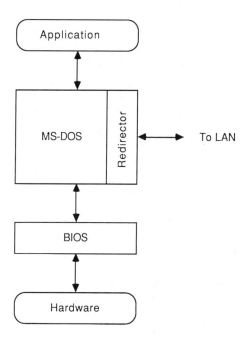

Fig. 13.3 — Relationship between MS-DOS and Redirector.

Although a separate entity, the Redirector can be thought of as part of MS-DOS, as shown in Fig. 13.3. It can also be considered to be a presentation layer service in OSI terms. Applications address the Redirector through a standard MS-DOS function call, and it in turn communicates with the NETBIOS interface by another MS-DOS call. Applications, therefore, do not necessarily know whether files are held locally or not, i.e. whether the Redirector is used or not. There are too many different function calls to describe here (Hurwitz (1985) lists most of them), but the two most relevant to the Redirector are *redirect device* and *cancel re-direction*, whose purposes are hopefully self-evident.

13.3   NETWORK OPERATING SYSTEMS

The functions of MS-DOS and NETBIOS described above provide the basic tools for the construction of what are known as *Network Operating Systems* (NOS), i.e. packages which permit the applications programmer to write network wide software independently of the network. Again, this is comparable to the support a normal operating system gives to the application programmer, making applications largely independent of the hardware. The two functions normally added to NETBIOS and MS-DOS are the file server and print spooling software, plus the necessary user interface and name management support.

There are several network operating systems on the market, not all of which are based on MS-DOS 3.1 and NETBIOS. The two described here represent the two extremes of the offerings. IBM's PC-Network Program is a very simple implementation based on MS-DOS, NETBIOS and the Redirector, whereas Novell's Netware, although based on MS-DOS, does not necessarily use either NETBIOS or the Redirector.

13.3.1   PC-Network Program

The PC-Network Program, originally produced by IBM for their PC-Network and then carried forward to the token ring, is a fairly basic product providing file serving, printer spooling, a simple PC-to-PC messaging system, and the relevant administration support. As can be seen from Fig. 13.4, it is implemented as a task which sits between the Redirector and NETBIOS, and it uses a protocol based on *Send Message Blocks* (SMB) to communicate with the remote server. The structure of the server is identical to that of the client PC, with the addition of a file server/spooler task.

The SMB protocol is relatively simple, comprising commands such as *START CONNECTION, OPEN FILE, READ BLOCK, WRITE BLOCK*, etc., which again are operating system independent. SMBs are generated by the Redirector, and because of the structure shown in Fig. 13.4, any PC on the LAN can be both a server and a client of other servers.

PC-Network Program has many limitations, however. First, the users must know the names of the servers and devices which they wish to access. Secondly all the protection mechanisms are based on access permissions for files or directories, there being no user names or passwords required to 'log-on' to the network. The main drawback, however, is the reliance on the NETBIOS naming scheme outlined above, which is very restrictive when multiple linked LANs are being constructed.

PC-Network Program uses the same building blocks as another network operating system, MS-NET (also from Microsoft), with the exception of NETBIOS, the functions of which MS-NET provides directly. The major difference between PC-Program and MS-NET, however, is that the MS-NET file server machine must be dedicated to the task — it cannot be used as

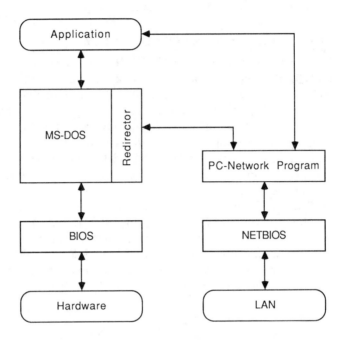

Fig. 13.4 — Schematic of software relationships in PC-Program station.

a workstation as well. MS-NET is the basis for many LAN operating systems, as Microsoft have not marketed it as an end product but have offered it to third party software producers to build more sophisticated services on top. Its main rival is Digital Research's DR-NET, which has been marketed in the same way. Many of the multiplicity of PC LAN systems in existence are based on either MS-NET or DR-NET.

13.3.2   Novell Netware

Novell's Netware system pre-dates NETBIOS and MS-DOS 3.1, but has now been updated under the name of Advanced Netware to take advantage of the enhanced MS-DOS features. It is one of the most portable Network Operating Systems, having been implemented on over 30 different LAN hardware systems.

Fig. 13.5 shows the structure of a server and a client Netware system. In place of the Redirector there is a *Netware shell*, which sits between DOS and the application. By 'stealing' an MS-DOS interrupt channel, the shell receives all the operating system commands, and decides if they are intended for the network or the local system. Local commands are passed to MS-DOS and remote commands to the *Internetwork Packet Exchange* (IPX), which passes them across the LAN to the server.

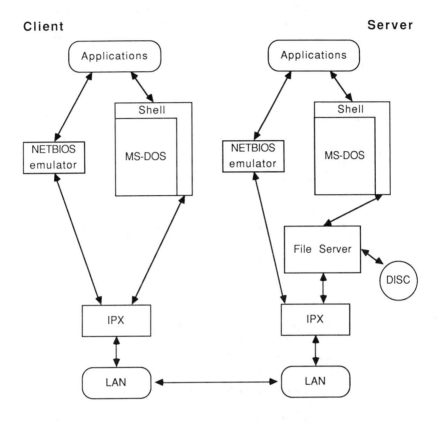

Fig. 13.5 — Typical Novell Netware client and server software relationships.

The system whereby the shell interprets commands, rather than MS-DOS, is more efficient for networked commands, and thus networked applications will run faster. In order to benefit from the many applications written to interface directly to NETBIOS, Novell also provide a NETBIOS emulator for the client station, and later releases of Advanced Netware also include Redirector support. Thus applications written for the PC-Network or for MS-NET will also run over Netware.

In a Netware server, the file server software is itself the operating system, and it does not use the MS-DOS disc driver. This enables Novell to format the disc differently, and to provide some enhanced disc driving operations. For example, directories are usually held in RAM, rather then being fetched from the disc each time, and the file server will not wait for the disc to respond to a write operation before it sends a reply to the client. Both these techniques greatly improve performance. It has also meant that Novell have been very quick to utilise the full memory and power of the Intel 80286-based PCs, as they are not restricted to the MS-DOS 640 Kbyte memory limitation. Although this would seem to imply that a file server must be dedicated to this task, MS-DOS can be run as a process under the Novell system to support local applications if required.

The Netware shell executes its remote operations using the Netware File Server Protocol (NFSP), which is similar in function to the SMB protocol outlined above. This is passed to the IPX handler, which is an implementation of the internetworking protocol originally developed by Xerox as part of its Xerox Network System (XNS) suite for use on Ethernet. IPX has been used by several Network Operating System developers, as it is designed to deal with multiple LANs. It is, however, proprietary and thus closed in the ISO sense.

At the user level, Netware requires user names and passwords to log on to the network, as well as providing file and directory level protection. Further examples of the advanced additional functionality provided by a network operating system are introduced by the latest version of Netware, called Fault Tolerant Netware. As its name suggests, this incorporates some new features designed to increase the reliability of the system, particularly the file server. Three levels of tolerance have been defined:

Level 1   This involves improved server software, specifically keeping backup copies of all the directories and performing 'read after write' checks on the disc. There are also various utilities for repairing damaged disc structures.

Level 2   At this level a second disc drive is added, which mirrors the first. Optionally the disc controller and power supplies can also be duplicated.

Level 3   This requires the addition of a complete duplicate of the file server, which should be physically located separately from the primary server. All operations to one are also performed on the other, and a transaction tracking system ensures that all operations are fully completed before being committed to the disc.

In the future, it is clear that network operating systems will be built above the standard protocols promoted by ISO. Novell, for example, have already indicated that this is their long term policy. In parallel it can be expected that many other functions will be added as the NOS vendors try to gain a larger share of a potentially enormous market.

13.4   IBM'S ADVANCED PROGRAM-TO-PROGRAM COMMUNICATION

There is, however, one other major supplier in the PC LAN market, and that is IBM itself. As mentioned above, when IBM's token ring product was announced, NETBIOS, the Send Message Block protocol and the PC-

Program were all brought forward from the PC-Network to run over the ring. IBM also announced, however, support for an extension to their wide area network protocol suite, Systems Network Architecture (SNA).

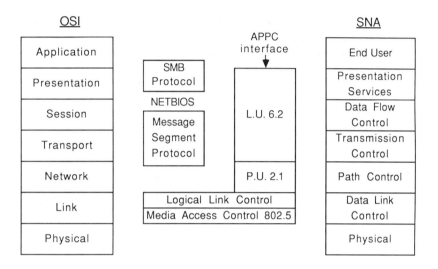

Fig. 13.6 — Relationship of SNA to ISO in IBM token ring station.

SNA has been around for a considerable time, being launched in 1974. It has a multi-layered structure, similar to the ISO model, as shown on the right hand side of Fig. 13.6. Until the launch of LU 6.2, however (LU stands for Logical Unit), SNA was very much a star oriented structure with a central computer polling all the other machines on its network. LU 6.2 is a true peer-to-peer protocol, which on the token ring runs over a network protocol called PU 2.1 (Physical Unit 2.1).

In a similar manner to the NETBIOS interface, IBM have defined a machine and operating system independent interface for use over LU 6.2, termed the *Advanced Program-to-Program Communication* (APPC) interface. This provides a set of functions to enable application programs to transfer information to other application programs. As Fig. 13.6 shows, APPC is thus an interface to a higher layer than NETBIOS in the hierarchy.

Fig. 13.7 shows the resultant software support available from IBM for the PC over the token ring. The MAC and LLC sublayers are provided on the LAN interface board, and the adapter handler software provides interfaces to both the LLC and the MAC layer, the direct interface. Alongside the NETBIOS program is the advanced program-to-program communications package, providing the support for SNA (LU 6.2) applications.

The first such application is the provision of PC based gateways to wide

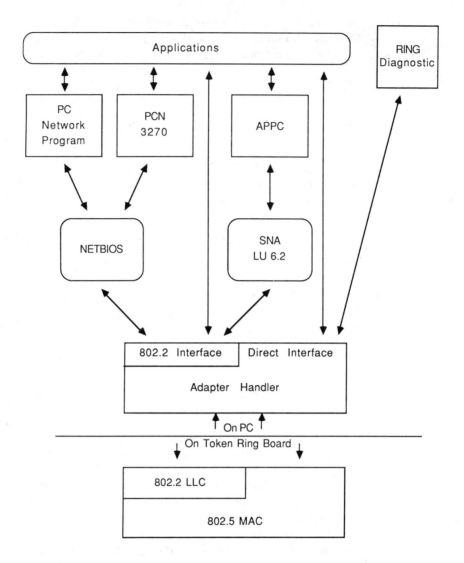

Fig. 13.7 — IBM-PC token ring software relationships.

area SNA networks, which will enable IBM mainframes to be interfaced to the ring. In addition, other applications, such as the rest of the ISO protocol set, could be implemented, though IBM have made no product announcements on that front. They have announced one application which uses the MAC sublayer directly, namely the ring diagnostics program. This provides a display and log of all hard and soft ring errors, and can test out any PC interface to the ring.

Part 5
Futures

The final part is concerned with current developments, many of which are not yet available to the end user, but which will affect the way existing LANs are used and which point the way to future LANs.

The first chapter in this part is concerned with extending existing LANs beyond their basic design limitations, and with the linking of LANs to other LANs and to wide area networks. The connection of LANs to existing networks is one of the main constraints to LAN market growth and is receiving considerable attention.

The next chapter is concerned with the often neglected subject of LAN management, from the nuts and bolts of installation to management systems which allow operations staff to control the network and investigate problems in an efficient manner.

The final chapter examines those developments in both hardware and software which will have a large impact in the next few years.

14

Extended LANS and internetworking

14.1 THE NEED FOR EXTENDED LANs

One of the clearest conclusions reached by many of the large organisations who have adopted LAN technology is that a single LAN is unlikely to satisfy the needs of all the user departments. There is still a desire for a unified approach to corporate networking, however, and this has resulted in the development of various ways of linking LANs, either within a local environment, which may be termed an *extended LAN*, or between widely separated sites, which is termed *internetworking*.

The reasons for adopting a system of multiple LANs can be divided into two main areas, the physical limitations of a given technology and the complexity of managing a large network.

14.1.1 Physical considerations

The physical properties of each of the ISO LANs and some PC LANs, in particular the strict limitations on distance covered and number of stations supported, have been described in Part 3. It is therefore clear that many large organisations will require more than one LAN, even of the same type, simply to cover the area required to reach the stations. With the IEEE 802.3 CSMA/CD LAN, for example, the 500 m segments can soon be used up in ducts and building risers as the cable is routed to pass within 50 m of each station. Although this problem could be solved in many cases by the installation of a broadband network, there are many instances where it is more economical to link several smaller LANS.

The second physical limitation usually encountered, particularly on some of the PC LANs, is the number of stations which may be attached. Even if the maximum number has not been reached it is often sensible to split the stations between two LANs in order to reduce the contention for the LAN between busy stations. This applies both to CSMA/CD LANs, where the number of collisions can rise alarmingly with the number of stations, and to token passing systems, where a station will have to wait longer for the token to rotate.

The final physical reason for using multiple LAN technologies is the suitability of the different access techniques to different departments within an organisation. For example, a process control plant normally requires a token passing scheme with guaranteed response times to commands, whereas a relatively simple LAN suffices to link word processors to printers.

14.1.2   Management considerations

The maintenance of a large LAN, indeed any large network, can pose considerable problems for a network manager. On a traditional wide area network the testing of equipment or tracing of a fault will normally affect only a small part of the network. Since in most LANs, however, the medium is shared this is often not the case. Thus dividing the network into smaller linked LANs simplifies the isolation of faults and the testing of new equipment.

It is also much simpler in management terms to add complete new LANs, to cover a new building for example, than to re-route the cable of an existing LAN. On most large networks there is a continuous round of equipment removal and resource reallocation. This may involve disruptions to departments which are not directly involved in the changes, but happen to share the same LAN. As a great deal of LAN traffic in practice tends to be local within departments, to a shared filestore say, rather than across departments, it is often simple to define sensible LAN boundaries.

Another management consideration is that the traffic requirements of one department may place an unnecessary cost on another. If, for example, a design office required fast graphics workstations with a suitably fast LAN to serve them, the decision to run the same LAN through all other departments may force the typing pool to install very expensive equipment, solely in order to attach to the fast LAN, where a simpler, cheaper LAN would suffice.

Finally, security is undoubtedly a major issue for many users. It is possible on some LANs, CSMA/CD for example, to monitor all the traffic on the LAN in a promiscuous mode, where a station can pick up all the packets, not just those addressed to that station. This is very useful for network monitoring purposes, but poses an obvious security risk. It may therefore be desirable to restrict secure data to its own individual LAN, but still permit some inter-LAN traffic.

There are three methods of extending LANs: *repeaters*, which operate at the OSI physical layer, *bridges*, which operate at the link layer (Fig. 14.1(a)), and *gateways*, which operate at the network layer (Fig. 14.1(b)). Gateways, which were briefly introduced in Chapter 11, are used to join dissimilar LANs or to link them to wide area networks, and they thus relate to the internetworking problem.

14.2   REPEATERS

As mentioned in Chapter 7, a repeater is a simple signal regenerator which can be used to extend the length of a bus topology LAN. The extended LAN operates as one network. For example, in the case of a CSMA/CD bus the signal plus all collisions passes through each repeater as if the cables had been butt-joined. Repeaters operate at the physical layer of the ISO model, and are used to join exactly identical LANs, being specific to each LAN. Even with the use of repeaters, however, there are still relatively low limits imposed on the number of segments and stations permitted.

(a) Bridge

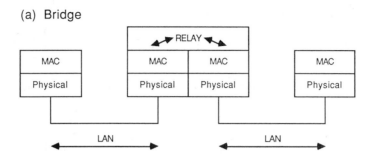

(b) Gateway

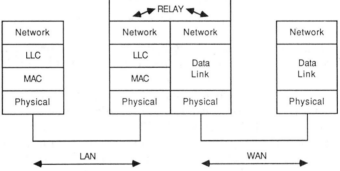

Fig. 14.1 — Functional schematics of bridge and gateway.

Repeaters can bestow other benefits, however. By using a fibre-optic link between repeaters, for example, two LAN segments can be linked over distances of a few kilometres. A repeater can also offer a degree of protection between a faulty segment and the rest of the network as it electrically isolates each segment. Cable breaks, for example, will only affect one segment.

14.3   BRIDGES

A bridge is a simple store-and-forward device, used to connect two or more LANs which use the same protocols above the MAC layer. As Fig. 14.2 illustrates, a bridge appears as a station on both LANs. One of the design features of IEEE LANs is that the MAC station addresses are all six bytes long, whatever the underlying physical LAN. Furthermore, all MAC frames carry both the source and destination addresses (see Figs 7.1, 8.2 and 9.2). Thus, by inspecting the source addresses in each of the packets on each side of the LAN, the bridge can build up two tables of station addresses, one for

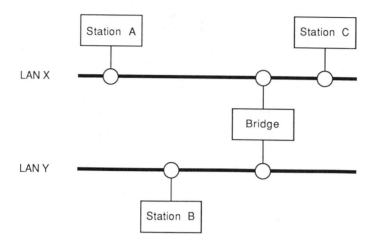

Fig. 14.2 — Local bridge configuration.

each side of the bridge. The bridge can then use these tables to decide if an incoming packet on one LAN needs to be passed to the other LAN, a process known as *forwarding*.

For example, when station A in Fig. 14.2 transmits a frame addressed to station B, the bridge will look up A's address first to check that it is in the table for LAN X, then it will look up B's address in the LAN X table, find that it is not there and therefore pass the packet through to LAN Y, using whatever LAN access technique is required by that LAN. If the transmission had been to station C, the bridge would not copy the packet onto the other LAN, unless C had not yet transmitted a frame (see below). The bridge copies the entire packet, including the original source address, onto the other LAN, using whatever access technique is required by that LAN. Therefore A, B and C all see each other as being on the same network, even though the underlying technology may be different on the two LANs.

The bridge can only record the position of a station when that station has transmitted a frame, i.e. when the source address has been detected. When a station starts up, any packets addressed to it must be passed through the bridge until it itself sends a frame. In this manner the bridge learns the whereabouts of the stations. Additional checks are also made to deal with a station being moved from one side of a bridge to the other, and most bridges will also remove addresses from the tables if the stations have not been active for some time. Most bridges also permit some form of user controlled restriction to be imposed, e.g. to switch off the learning process and permit only packets from certain specified stations to be passed through the bridge.

Obviously a bridge introduces a bottleneck into the LAN system. It usually consists of two processors, one handling each LAN, plus a large amount of common memory to buffer the packets. In practice, since the bridge has very little processing to do, quite impressive performance figures can be achieved. At present most bridges are restricted to CSMA/CD to

CSMA/CD LANs, as these have existed longest, and two performance parameters are quoted. The first is the filtering rate, i.e. the maximum number of packets per second existing on one LAN which the bridge is able to examine, to see if they need to be passed through to the other LAN. Typical filtering rates are of the order of several thousand packets per second for CSMA/CD. The second parameter is the forwarding rate, i.e. the maximum number of packets which a bridge can pass through, assuming a lightly loaded target LAN. This figure is usually around one or two thousand packets per second. Thus it can be seen that a carefully divided LAN linked by a bridge, with each section carrying mainly local traffic, can be implemented with little or no performance degradation.

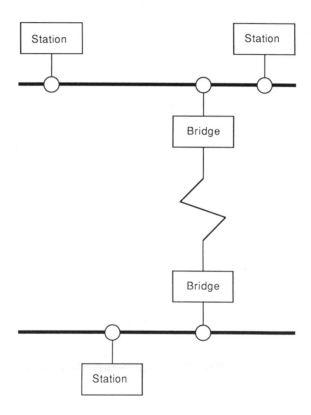

Fig. 14.3 — Remote bridge configuration.

The bridge shown in Fig.14.2 is termed a *local bridge*, i.e. the two LANs must be physically close to each other as the bridge must satisfy the station attachment constraints for each LAN (50 m for CSMA/CD, for example). A bridge can, however, be divided into two halves, with some form of point-to-point communications link between them, for example a fibre optic cable or a synchronous connection across a national network (Fig. 14.3). Thus *remote bridges* can enable LANs to be joined into one logical network stretching the length of the country. Of course the inter-bridge link may operate at much lower speeds than either LAN, but the filtering of the packets can cut down the traffic to acceptable limits.

In theory the number of LANs being linked by either local or remote bridges or a combination of the two can be extended indefinitely. In practice, however, care must be taken that the time required for a packet to cross many LANs and bridges does not exceed the re-transmission timeouts built into the higher levels of protocol. Furthermore, since bridges perform no error correction (being designed to ignore any packet in error), the higher protocol layers must recover from any bridge induced error, such as failing to pick up a packet because of high loads.

A variant of the remote bridge is the *router*, which carries the MAC frames over a switched wide area network, e.g. an X.25 based WAN, rather than over a dedicated point-to-point link (Fig. 14.4). The route over the

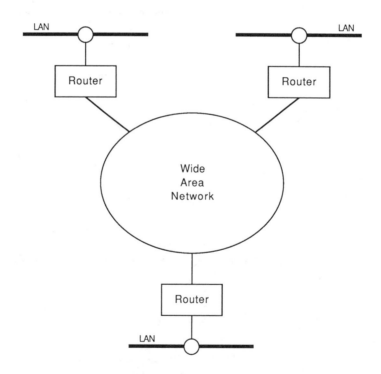

Fig. 14.4 — Example of a network using routers.

WAN can either be established by manual control of the bridge, or where IP is being run on the LAN, the destination IP address can be used to route over the network to a similar router. This is very close to the gateway function described below, with the difference that communication is restricted to router to router traffic, i.e. LAN station to LAN station, and not LAN station to WAN station.

14.4   IEEE MAC BRIDGE STANDARDS

Although Figs 14.2 and 14.3 show two-port bridges, i.e. bridges which can link two LANs only, bridges can be multi-port and can thus be used to form very complex 'networks of LANs' incorporating redundant bridges and alternative routes, as shown in Fig. 14.5. With such schemes there needs to

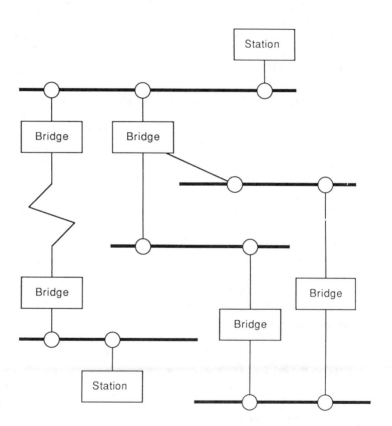

Fig. 14.5 — Example of a complex multi-bridge network.

be some control over the bridges to ensure that only one bridge is actively passing packets between any two LANs, otherwise broadcast and multicast packets would loop around the system indefinitely.

The IEEE Project 802.1 committee has been addressing this problem and has produced a specification (IEEE 1986), currently at the draft stage, for MAC bridges between IEEE LANs. The specification is in two parts, one covering the management of bridges, the other defining an algorithm for dealing with the multiple routes problem — the *spanning tree algorithm*.

14.4.1   The spanning tree algorithm

The objective of the spanning tree algorithm is to reduce the topology of the network of LANs to a single tree structure, which spans all of the LANs and ensures that there is only one active path between any two stations. The algorithm is designed such that the bridges will configure themselves in a relatively short time, and provide fault tolerance in the event of a bridge failing. It will also quickly and automatically accommodate any new bridge which is inserted into the system, a repaired bridge for example.

Although still under development, and of considerable complexity, the algorithm is worthy of brief description. It is implemented by an inter-bridge protocol which runs over the LLC Class 1 link layer. The initial requirements are that each bridge, and each port within each bridge, is given a unique identifier and that each bridge is given a unique priority level within the system.

The algorithm first selects one bridge to be the *root* of the tree. The identifier of this bridge is then passed using a reserved multicast address to every other bridge in the network. The objective of the algorithm is to select a *designated active bridge* for each LAN, with the ports within the designated bridge becoming the designated port for the route between the LANs. This is achieved by computing the *cost* of the path between any port in a bridge and the root bridge. The cost is passed to all the bridges on a given LAN, and any port which has a cost higher than another will be closed.

In the example shown in Fig. 14.6, where bridge A is the root, port X of bridge E on LAN 4 will have a lower path cost than either port Z of bridge E, or port X of bridge F. Thus port X of bridge E will be the active port on LAN 4. If two ports have the same path cost, for example in bridges B and C on LAN 3, then the bridge with the higher priority will become the designated bridge. The path costs are computed by the root bridge periodically sending out packets which pass through each bridge in the system, including bridges which are not currently the designated bridge for a LAN. Each bridge will forward these packets, adding on the individual port path costs through each port on the bridge. Thus an incoming packet will inform a bridge of the cost of that route to the port, and any new path which comes into play will automatically be taken into account in the cost calculation, the designated bridges and ports changing to take account of the new paths.

The individual port costs are pre-set to reflect, for example, the difference between a high speed route, such as local bridge B in Fig 14.6, and a slower remote bridge, such as bridge D. Thus, after the operation of the algorithm, the active designated bridges will be as shown in Fig. 14.7. All of the bridges in the system maintain timers, first to ensure that the root bridge is continuing to send out path packets, and secondly to ensure that the designated bridge on any LAN is still active. Should any timer expire, the bridges will recompute their position and restructure the tree.

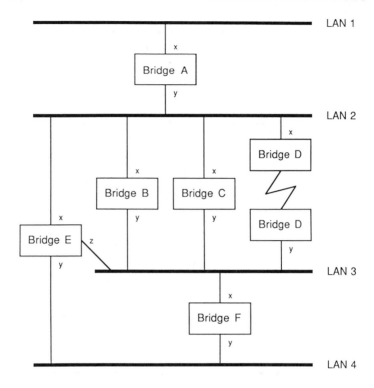

Fig. 14.6 — Example of spanning tree algorithm bridged network.

14.4.2 Bridge management

The second element of the IEEE specification relates to the management of the bridges in an extended LAN. When a network may stretch over many LANs, possibly many miles apart, it is very important for the network manager to be able to control the operation of the bridges. The IEEE recommendations form part of their overall network management strategy, outlined in the next chapter. For bridges, however, five categories of management facility have been defined, as follows:

> *Configuration management* covers the allocation of identifiers to, bridges and ports, the ability to initialise, reset and close down a bridge remotely, the control of individual ports on a bridge, and the ability to force a re-computation of the spanning tree described above.
> *Fault management* includes the detection and reporting of bridge, failures, including the dumping of bridge memory (sending the contents of the memory to a management station when a bridge fails). It also includes diagnostic testing and the maintenance of error logs.
> *Performance management* involves the collection and reporting of performance and traffic statistics, both of an individual bridge and through the operation of the spanning tree algorithm.
> *Security management* includes access controls, encryption and the ability to control the address learning process of the bridge.

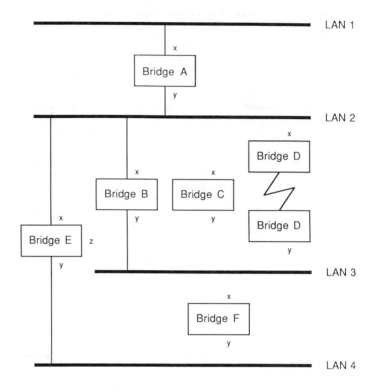

Fig. 14.7 — Network as in Fig. 14.6 showing designated bridges.

Accounting management facilities are included by the IEEE for further, study. They relate to the recording of any costs incurred by the use of a bridge resource.

The IEEE specification defines such items as the structure of the filtering database, and the inter-bridge protocol commands which are to be used to implement the management features.

14.5   GATEWAYS

The term *gateway* is used to describe several essentially different entities, which basically perform the same function, that of linking different networks together.

14.5.1   ISO and general gateways

In ISO terms, as already introduced in Chapter 11 and at the beginning of this chapter, a gateway operates at the network layer (Fig. 14.1), and it is used to link different addressing domains or significantly different technologies, e.g. LAN to WAN. The first three layers on each side of an ISO gateway may be different on either side, but the transport layer and above are carried on both sides (Fig. 11.8), between the end systems.

The second type of gateway connects networks which run very different protocols on either side. This may be between two LANs, LAN to WAN, or between two WANs. It implies a great deal of *protocol conversion* work within the gateway to interpret the packets on each side. This is the approach being taken by IBM, with the provision of protocol converters at each of the SNA layers to map onto the ISO layers (Routt 1987). This is possible because of the roughly equal layering between the two schemes (Fig. 13.6), but it would obviously be much more difficult with dissimilar protocol systems such as TCP/IP to ISO.

This approach presents several major problems, however. Even with the relatively simple ISO gateway, where only three layers are involved, the conversions required, possibly involving different packet sizes on each side, can be time-consuming. Thus gateways tend to be much more complex and expensive than bridges. When several layers of protocol conversion are involved, the problems are magnified greatly. Protocol conversion presents some problems, in that there are inevitably some features available on one side of the gateway which cannot be mapped onto the protocol on the other side. The gateway must decide if such cases should result in an error being flagged. In general, passing through a protocol converter usually involves a loss of facilities.

There are also often significant timing differences between protocols, particularly between a LAN and a WAN. For example, to return to the LLC Type 2 protocol described in Chapter 11, the timing between RR packets on an idle link is usually quite slow on a wide area network, but may be very fast on a LAN. This can result in a build-up within the gateway, unless the gateway suppresses the excess. Retry timers at the higher layers, whereby a station assumes that a packet has gone astray and tries to re-transmit it, can also cause problems between a fast and a slow network.

One of the most serious problems to be solved when linking dissimilar networks is that of enabling stations on one to address stations on the other when the style of station addressing is different. This usually results in large tables of addresses in each gateway, which may be difficult to maintain on very large networks.

The final problem is that of error reporting: how, for example, does a gateway report the failure of a wide area virtual circuit connection to a connectionless LAN station?

14.5.2   PC-LAN gateways

The final type of gateway, and currently the type which is most widely available and in use, connects PC-LANs. PC-LAN gateways can be divided into two classes, each of which provides the same two types of connection capability. First, a PC itself can be used as a gateway, normally by the addition of a board which will provide *terminal emulation*, often of only one terminal, to the wide area network. The second class is a dedicated gateway which will usually provide several connections to the WAN.

Each class can be used in two ways. Fig. 14.8 shows the simplest, in which the gateway provides a number of asynchronous lines to a PAD, or (more

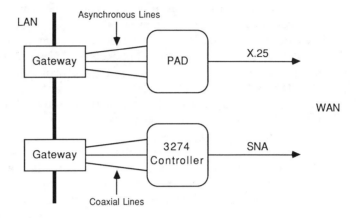

Fig. 14.8 — Example of terminal emulation gateways.

commonly in the PC-LAN market) a number of coaxial lines to an IBM 3274 terminal controller. This method is usually relatively limited, with the gateway emulating terminals as far as the wide area network is concerned. In the simplest case the LAN user may have to connect to the gateway and then connect again to the desired host on the WAN, i.e. the gateway will not be *transparent* to the end user. The degree of higher functionality available, such as file transfer, will depend on the type of emulation supported and the availability of such services to terminals on the wide area network. Such gateways are usually lightly loaded, however, and if the gateway is PC-based it may be possible to use the PC simultaneously as a workstation.

The second method is for the gateway to emulate an entire PAD or 3274 controller, and therefore connect to the WAN by a synchronous line (Fig. 14.9). This is a more complex gateway, as the wide area protocols have to be

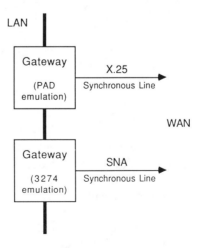

Fig. 14.9 — Example of PAD/controller emulation gateways.

implemented, but will normally provide better performance at a reasonable cost, and will be transparent to the user.

Many current PCs which are attached to LANs are also connected directly to corporate mainframes or networks by individual terminal emulation boards. This is both an expensive and under-utilised system, and it is predicted (PC Week 1987) that PC-LAN gateways are potentially the largest LAN growth area over the next few years.

15

Network management

LAN network management has tended to be a slightly ignored field until recently, the inference being that most of the PC-LANs are so simple and reliable that not much management is required. As LANs have become larger, however, with many segments and stations supplied from different vendors spread over a large area, the importance of management has been recognised. Network management can be divided into three parts, installation and configuration, monitoring and diagnostics, and security.

15.1 INSTALLATION AND CONFIGURATION

Although most complex LANs will be installed by specialist companies and tested using their own equipment, it is essential for the end user to be involved in the planning of the system. For more modest LANs, the installation and subsequent administration will probably be undertaken in-house, but it should be noted that this will almost certainly require the appointment of a full time LAN manager, and will most definitely require an investment in training courses and in time.

The planning of cable routes should not only comply with any limitations that the LAN itself may impose, but should also take into account the reasons described in the previous chapter for dividing the network into linked parts. Some cables are very bulky and require a set minimum bending radius for turning a corner. Thus cable trays can rapidly be filled up. Another early consideration should be the placement of equipment, such as repeaters or wiring concentrators, which may need a power supply and will need to be accessible for maintenance. Vital components should not be too accessible, however, as this will provide more opportunities for accidental disruption to the network, by well intentioned personnel switching off power sockets, for example. Another problem to be taken into account when positioning equipment, particularly CSMA/CD transceivers, is their considerable weight and bulk. Although designed to tap onto the cable, some transceivers are so heavy as to distort the cable, and these must be supported in some way.

Good physical installation cannot be stressed too highly, especially for systems such as CSMA/CD, where a badly installed transceiver can disrupt the whole network. For larger installations, a *time domain reflectometer* should be purchased. This checks the continuity of the cable and the validity of the transceivers, and should be used by an installer to validate the installation, as it can rapidly pin-point physical damage to the cable. Electrical safety is also a concern in large LAN systems, particularly where cables are being stretched between buildings. Apart from the fact that the earth potentials may be different, causing an unwanted current to flow along the cable, there is also a risk of very large induced surges caused by lightning strikes, unless suitable precautions have been taken. As mentioned in Chapter 7, ECMA have produced a useful document (ECMA 97) which addresses LAN safety.

Once a LAN's physical components have been installed and tested, the LAN manager is normally required to configure the components on the LAN to suit local requirements. In the case of file servers, this normally involves the details of which PCs or users are to access which partition of the file server's discs. Furthermore, many LANs use network interface units and gateways which will require their configurations to be set up at the time of installation. For an individual RS-232 port this can imply many parameters, and a large network can take several days to configure.

Two of the most important aspects to be taken into account when choosing a LAN are its ease of configurability and the amount of information available to the installer when the configuration is found to be faulty. Many systems have some form of centralised network manager where configurations are carried out and from where stations are loaded. It is essential that this system be easy to use and be well protected from unauthorised users. It is perhaps a comment on existing LANs that there is a small but thriving industry providing 'add-on' software to present the user with a simplified method of configuring the LAN. A further aspect to be considered is that, like all other software, LAN software will require to be updated from time to time with new releases from the supplier. This can often require some reconfiguration and will mean the reloading of every station on the network, which may take a considerable time.

Another often neglected aspect of LAN installation is the training of the system's users. Such users, particularly of PCs, will be used to stand-alone working, with local resources under their own control. To get the best out of any LAN system, the people using it must be aware of how it works, in general terms at least: what facilities it offers, and how to report any problems they may experience. It is also frequently the case that the transfer of single user applications to LAN wide applications is not simple, and as in the case of the LAN manager a large investment of time and money in training may be necessary.

Finally, good record keeping, both for the configuration details and the physical location of cables and taps, is highly advisable. This will make any additions to the network much easier to plan, as well as enabling mainten-ance engineers to find faulty components quickly.

15.2   MONITORING AND DIAGNOSTICS

Once a LAN has been correctly installed and configured, it is essential to have the proper tools to monitor its performance and to detect faults quickly and accurately. Some networks offer performance measurement and statistics gathering within the management station, but there is now a growing market for independent monitoring devices, particularly for CSMA/CD LANs which have been on the market longer.

These typically can inspect all of the packets on the LAN, by receiving in promiscuous mode, and can thus display the overall loading on the network. The more sophisticated models may offer station by station loading figures, which are very useful for planning purposes. Such figures can also give early warnings of faults developing, on individual transceivers for example. Monitors also report all errors detected and may offer simple validation tests to ensure that all the stations are operable. Another important feature for CSMA/CD LANs is the measurement of collisions, which can indicate when the network is becoming too highly loaded, and should thus be split using bridges. On token passing LANs the monitor can show the occurrence of lost tokens and the degree of utilisation of each of the priority levels, which may point to a more efficient allocation of station priorities.

The other main feature of LAN monitors is that they can capture, display and interpret the packets transmitted on the LAN, usually under some form of user-imposed filtering, to trace all packets to or from a specified station. This is of most value when debugging new protocol implementations, but could be useful, for instance, when trying to find out the reason for a newly added station, which supposedly runs the correct protocols, not in practice doing so. Protocol interpretation is also used to detect high occurrences of retransmissions, or duplicated packets at the higher protocol levels.

This feature of the monitor, however, presents a major security problem in the wrong hands, as packets can be scanned to pick up confidential data such as passwords. A potentially disruptive feature, although also very useful for load testing, is the ability to generate test packets, targeted at specific stations and containing specific data, at very high data rates. The accidental flooding of the network, or at least of one station, is a real possibility with a powerful monitor. For example, several CSMA/CD monitors are capable of single-handedly loading the LAN with traffic at almost 100% of the LAN's theoretical throughput.

Many PC-LANs offer some form of diagnostic facility to test the integrity of the network and may also permit a degree of remote control over the facilities; e.g. control of user access to particular services. The existence of a network control centre to provide such facilities largely depends on the manufacturer at present, and tends to reflect what is being offered in the wide area network arena. A few manufacturers do offer very sophisticated network management centres, and some are planning to use Artificial Intelligence based systems in the future. The main developments are likely to come from the standardisation bodies; this work, along with IBM's network management system, is described in 15.4 and 15.5 below.

15.3 SECURITY

One of the advantages of having many separate PCs in an organisation is that the data held on each is under the direct control of the user. Very sensitive data can be held in safes, and only loaded onto the machine when required. The networking of PCs, or any systems in an open environment, raises concerns about the continued security of data, and future network management systems will have to address the issue.

Security issues can be categorised into three classes. The first is *access control*, i.e. the checking of user authorisation to use the network itself or the individual resources of the network. Most LANs rely on restricting access to specific sections of a filestore's disc, although a few request a user password. Many of the general purpose LANs assume that the end systems themselves are taking responsibility for user access to those systems, whether over the LAN or not.

The second security issue is that of *crash recovery*, i.e. the successful recovery from a failure of any part of the LAN or its attached resources. This is particularly important when PCs are dependent upon a filestore. Previous chapters have illustrated some of the techniques used to prevent data loss, such as mirroring the filestore or using fault tolerant software.

The final aspect of security, which may concern some users, is that of deliberate or accidental *eavesdropping* in order to capture packets which may contain sensitive data, such as passwords. One of the advantages of the traditional switched network was that to monitor traffic a line had to be broken, if only briefly, to insert a monitor. That monitor could then only examine the traffic on the one line. With a LAN, as noted above, a monitor can be inserted at any tapping point, without disruption, and is then able to monitor all the traffic on the network. It may even be possible in some workstations to program the station to collect the packets which are not addressed to it, or even to pretend to be another station.

Two suggested approaches to eavesdropping problems which have attracted attention to date involve either organisational change or the use of additional hardware. In the first instance one individual in an organisation should be appointed to have overall responsibility for LAN security, with the authority to cross the many departmental boundaries to which the LAN may provide service. If security is a major concern then the encryption of data on the LAN may be a solution. There is no universal guide to encryption, and although encryption has been defined to be a feature of the presentation layer of the ISO model, there is still some debate as to whether data at the other levels should also be encrypted. This is most efficiently done by additional hardware encryption techniques.

15.4 IEEE LAN MANAGEMENT STANDARDS

Unfortunately most manufacturers have invented their own network management support, ranging from very complex, comprehensive, facilities to the minimum required to configure the network. One such system, IBM's

Netview, is described in 15.5 below. Management has not, however, been neglected by the standardisation bodies, even though their priority to date has been to produce working LANs.

One of the most advanced proposals, which may form the basis for future ISO work, has come from the IEEE's Project 802.1 committee (IEEE 1987). This proposes a standard for LAN management which will enable a station bought from one manufacturer to be configured and controlled from another's network management station. The proposal is at an early stage, but a working draft has been published from which it is possible to extract the principles upon which it is based.

As can be seen from Fig. 15.1, the proposal is based on the OSI reference

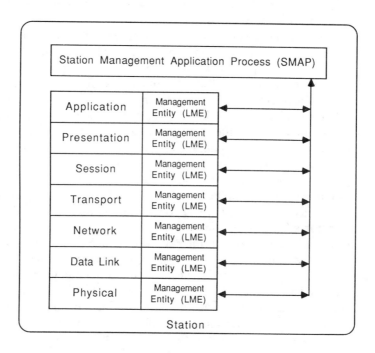

Fig. 15.1 — Structure of IEEE network management proposals.

model. At each level there is a *Layer Management Entity* (LME) which is responsible for the gathering of statistics at that layer and for the effecting of access control and activation commands for that layer. For example, it should be possible to restrict the number of simultaneous sessions, or to reset the count of packets retransmitted at the LLC layer.

Each station also contains a *Station Management Application Process* (SMAP), which is responsible for controlling the activities of the LMEs. It is also capable of communicating with other SMAPs and with any number of central network control centres. This communication will take place using the ISO protocols already in place, although an additional management protocol will also be required. The SMAP will also be responsible for the down line loading of the station and for any store dumping should the station crash.

The various IEEE committees for each LAN (see Chapter 10) are currently defining the actions which will be required, and the statistics which should be gathered for the specific MAC and LLC layers. It will, however, be some time before the exact details are agreed and management products appear. In an attempt to fill the gap, IBM has launched its own network management system, known as Netview.

15.5   IBM's NETVIEW MANAGEMENT SYSTEM

IBM are one of the major companies who have designed their own network management software to control their proprietary wide area networks, SNA in IBM's case. Early in 1986, IBM announced an amalgam of and extension to their existing products under the name *Netview*. Netview runs on an IBM mainframe and provides a statistical display of and control over an SNA-based network. What is of more significance for LANs is the second announcement, in late 1986, of *Netview/PC*, which placed some of the Netview functions onto an IBM-PC.

Netview/PC is intended to link the network management machine on an IBM token ring into the corporate network management system (Fig. 15.2).

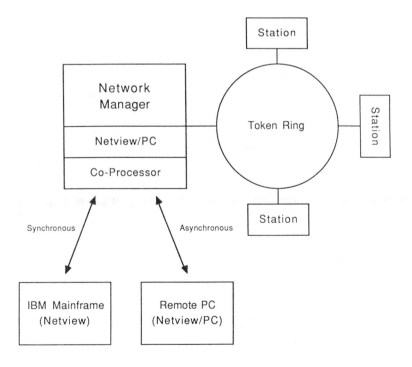

Fig. 15.2 — Schematic of Netview/PC system.

It can also link a LAN manager to a remote PC. The significance of the Netview products is that IBM have published the interface to the system within the IBM-PC, and thus are encouraging other LAN manufacturers to base their own network management systems on top of IBM's communications and mainframe support.

15.5.1   Netview

The Netview software, which runs in the mainframe, is designed to control SNA network resources. It performs two basic functions: monitoring the network hardware, including such items as modems if they are equipped to respond to Netview's control messages; and monitoring SNA sessions in order to produce, for example, billing information. The information from both types of monitoring can be presented to a network control display. Although Netview can only control IBM devices at present, it is IBM's intention to permit other suppliers who wish to use Netview to control their own devices from the mainframe.

15.5.2   Netview/PC

At the PC, Netview consists of additional software and hardware. The hardware is a coprocessor which handles all of the communications with the mainframe or remote PC. This is based on the LU 6.2 protocol mentioned in Chapter 13.

The software structure is shown in Fig. 15.3. The crucial interface is the

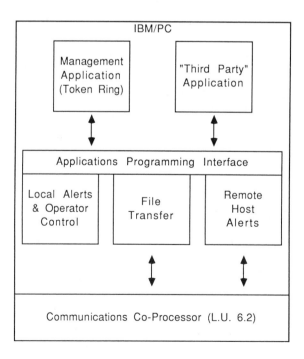

Fig. 15.3 — Simplified schematic of Netview/PC software.

Applications Programming Interface (API), which is what IBM has published. It supports several features, namely the sending of alerts to the remote host, local operator control, the sending of large amounts of data to the remote hosts, which is effectively a file transfer system for MS-DOS files, and finally a facility for the interpretation of messages sent from the remote host.

Thus IBM intend to supply the infrastructure for network management, while leaving the suppliers free to design their own style of management. One of the first third party packages has come from Rolm, the PABX manufacturers, who are owned by IBM. Their system links into the call logging facilities of the PABX, and can thus provide a status display for the voice system on the central mainframe.

The principal drawback of the Netview system, however, is that the user is required to have an IBM mainframe to gain the full facilities, and this may militate against it in favour of the IEEE system in the long term.

16

Future trends in local area networks

16.1 FUTURE OPEN SYSTEMS STANDARDS

It is already clear that the International Standards Organisation's efforts to produce open systems interconnection standards have a great deal of support in official Government circles in many countries. The United States government, for example, which has an estimated IT budget of $16 thousand million per year, has drafted a Government OSI Procurement document (GOSIP), which may become mandatory in future government systems specifications. Manufacturers are also grouping together to speed up the development of the standards, notably within the Corporation for Open Systems, which contains all the major US manufacturers, and is now linking with the European Standards Promotion and Applications Group (SPAG), and the Japanese Promotion Conference for OSI (POSI).

The major problem, however, is that there are already in excess of 30 ISO standards which have reached at least the draft stage, plus a similar number in production. As noted earlier, each of these standards may have several classes, and within each class many options, such that even when two systems claim to conform to the same protocols they may not be able to interwork. This problem is being addressed by the above groups and others, with the resultant promotion of *functional standards*.

16.1.1 Functional standards

A functional standard is a set of detailed recommendations, usually based on the ISO protocols, defining how one or more of the standards should be used in combination to meet a particular requirement or function. In general a functional standard ties down the details of which options shall be used within which protocol class for a given layer of the model. It normally comprises a list of specifications for each layer, i.e. a vertical slice through the OSI model. This is known as a *protocol stack*, and will fill in many of the details which the basic standards leave to the implementor. For example, many protocols do not specify maximum data field sizes, but this can be crucial for good performance.

The agreement of many manufacturers to adopt a functional standard has many advantages. First, it provides a stable development environment: even when some standards are in draft form it is possible to select a stable subset for implementation and thus provide early practical experience of a protocol. Second, it greatly simplifies the conformance testing problem. If two products conform to a functional standard, then they will be guaranteed to interwork *for that function*, e.g. for document interchange, but not necessarily for any other function.

In Europe the lead for this work has been taken by the CEN/CENELEC manufacturers' groups, along with the CEPT, the grouping of European PTTs. They have produced a set of ENs (European Norms) which specify not only which protocol options to use, but also the tests for conformance which any product will have to undergo before being able to claim conformance to the standard set. Unlike most other functional standards, ENs do not normally define an entire protocol stack, but concentrate on individual layers of the model. One very relevant standard for LANs, for example, is numbered T/611 and concerns the use of CSMA/CD LANs within the Connection Oriented Network Service.

In the USA, functional standards have been developed from two different sources. The National Bureau of Standards (NBS) has produced a functional standard for the message handling application called OSINET, in much the same way as the European efforts. Secondly two major users, General Motors and Boeing, have, by virtue of their vast purchasing power, been able to specify two sets of standards, MAP and TOP. These have generated great interest, as they are unique in being defined by users, rather than by manufacturers or standardisation bodies.

16.1.2 Manufacturing automation protocol

MAP, the *Manufacturing Automation Protocol* (MAP 2.1 1985), is a set of proposals originally promoted by General Motors, who were faced with the problem of automating their factories. As in the computer communications arena, the manufacturers of process control and robotic equipment were each locked into their own methods of communications, largely based on point-to-point links. Thus large manufacturers, like General Motors, had a mixture of separate partly communicating devices, which could only interwork by the development of very complex gateways, between what General Motors termed 'islands of automation'.

In 1980, therefore, General Motors set up a task force to study their existing factory automation procedures and recommend alternatives. The task force discovered that a large part of the factory cost was in practice computer communications, as most automation equipment was computer based. They therefore concluded that costs would be reduced, cables eliminated, maintenance simplified and productivity increased if all automated equipment were attached to interconnected LANs, and all ran the same software.

The result was the production of a functional standard in the form of a vertical protocol stack, as shown in Fig. 16.1(a). They decided on a bus topology, as this is simpler to wire round a factory, and the token passing access method, as this could guarantee the timed delivery of messages which is necessary for process control. Thus the MAC layer was chosen to be the IEEE 802.4 token bus, using the two channel 10 Mbit/s option. The use of

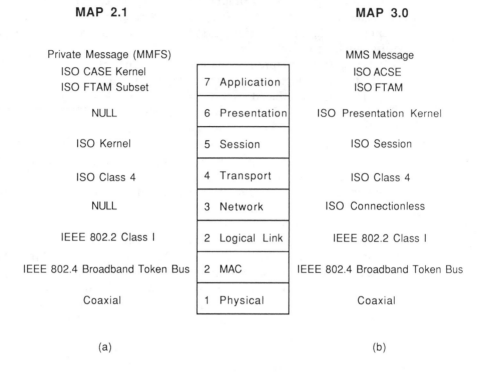

MAP 2.1   MAP 3.0

MAP 2.1	Layer	MAP 3.0
Private Message (MMFS) ISO CASE Kernel ISO FTAM Subset	7 Application	MMS Message ISO ACSE ISO FTAM
NULL	6 Presentation	ISO Presentation Kernel
ISO Kernel	5 Session	ISO Session
ISO Class 4	4 Transport	ISO Class 4
NULL	3 Network	ISO Connectionless
IEEE 802.2 Class I	2 Logical Link	IEEE 802.2 Class I
IEEE 802.4 Broadband Token Bus	2 MAC	IEEE 802.4 Broadband Token Bus
Coaxial	1 Physical	Coaxial

(a)   (b)

Fig. 16.1 — MAP 2.0 and 3.0 protocol stacks.

broadband also enables factory video security and environment monitoring systems to be carried on the same cable. The MAP specification is intended, however, to be media independent, and thus baseband MAP networks are possible.

General Motors then selected the protocols and services, and the options within the protocols, at each layer of the ISO model from what ISO had defined at the time. This early stack was identical to Fig. 16.1(a), with the exception that the network layer was left as null. The stack shown, known as MAP 2.1, was soon produced, and has become the first generally available set of protocols. The MMFS protocol (Manufacturing Message Format Standard), is a non-ISO protocol which was in use within General Motors for driving some devices.

Since General Motors have a budget of several thousand million dollars to devote to factory automation over the next few years, many manufacturers have been keen to develop products, and many other users are keen to adopt any standard which presents itself. The potential success of the approach has been demonstrated, firstly at the US Autofact show in November 1985 when 21 different suppliers took part in a demonstration of interworking. By the end of 1986, a similar demonstration at the UK's CIMAP show involved no less than 60 co-operating companies.

Not all manufacturers and users have jumped onto the MAP bandwagon yet, however, as there are two main problems. First MAP is not static, but is still developing along with the ISO protocols, and the projected MAP 3.0 will not be compatible with MAP 2.1 as it will replace the MMFS protocol with another called RS511. Second, current MAP installations, being broadband based, are expensive compared with other LANs, and manufacturers are concerned that smaller users will not be willing to pay the necessary start-up costs.

There is also a rival, European-based, grouping of manufacturers and users, called the Communications Network for Manufacturing Applications (CNMA), which are promoting a different MAP 3.0 stack. This is shown as Fig. 16.1(b), and shows the inclusion of more of the ISO higher layers, plus yet another message passing protocol, called MMS (Manufacturing Message Service). As these message protocols are responsible for the delivery of the driving commands to the automated equipment, they are obviously crucial to the future success of MAP. There is, however, an International Federation of MAP User Groups, which hopes to impose a single version of MAP 3.0.

CNMA are also promoting a 'collapsed architecture' version of MAP, known as EPA (Enhanced Performance Architecture), in which layers 3 to 6 inclusive would be removed completely when used within a very local network, as they will be superfluous. Furthermore, because there are relatively few broadband networks in Europe and a great many baseband LANs already installed in factories, they are suggesting the option of running the protocol set over the IEEE 802.3 CSMA/CD bus. It can therefore be seen that, even with a strongly promoted functional specification, there will be a considerable settling down period before true interworking is achieved.

One final benefit of MAP is that it is intended that all the computer based communications of an organisation, including terminals and computing resources, be attached to the one cable, as well as programmable machine tools. This is forcing many organisations to rethink, or determine for the first time, their corporate communications requirements, an exercise which should result in improvements throughout the organisation.

16.1.3   Technical and office protocol

TOP, which stands for *Technical and Office Protocol* (TOP 1985), is another application-specific protocol stack based on the ISO model. It addresses the area of office systems, particularly technical office work which requires advanced graphics. The initiative for TOP came from the Boeing company, and they have since been joined by General Motors, Ford Motors and others. The TOP choice of protocols is shown in Fig. 16.2. Although the work is not as far advanced as the MAP developments, indications are that many manufacturers are interested.

The main differences between MAP and TOP are at the MAC layer, which for TOP is the CSMA/CD bus, and at the *message* passing application level, which for TOP is the CCITT X.400 protocol, which is the forerunner of the ISO protocol for message passing. As there are obviously some

TOP

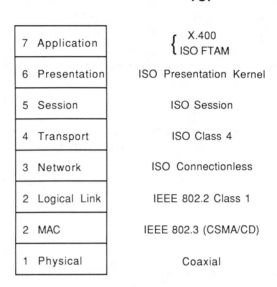

7 Application	⎰ X.400 ⎱ ISO FTAM
6 Presentation	ISO Presentation Kernel
5 Session	ISO Session
4 Transport	ISO Class 4
3 Network	ISO Connectionless
2 Logical Link	IEEE 802.2 Class 1
2 MAC	IEEE 802.3 (CSMA/CD)
1 Physical	Coaxial

Fig. 16.2 — TOP protocol stack.

installations with a need for both MAP and TOP, there is every possibility of some common subsets being defined in the future, or even a total merger of the two.

Even with the above efforts in functional standards, it can be seen that there is much room for confusion, and ISO themselves have announced a new initiative to try to clarify the situation. They are proposing that regional workshops convene to produce proposals for *International Standardisation Profiles* (ISPs). ISPs will list those options from within the ISO standards which *must* be implemented for specific applications. They will thus form a functional standard of functional standards. Because of the regional differences of approach, however, particularly between Europe and the USA, there is a possibility that more than one ISP could exist for a single application.

16.2 FUTURE HARDWARE

The one certainty concerning the future development of LANs is that the technology will not stand still. In particular there is now a considerable blurring of the categories of LAN, particularly with regard to topologies and media (outlined in Part 2), and this can be expected to continue. To take two recent examples, experiments have taken place, and a few products announced, in running 10 Mbit/s CSMA/CD over ordinary twisted pair cable, rather than the more expensive coaxial cable (Howe 1987). This would permit the use of existing telephone wiring, in the same way as the StarLAN network, but at ten times the speed.

The second example of this blurring of dividing lines is the linking of broadband networks by joining the headends in a star configuration. This is particularly being promoted for MAP, as the star configuration reduces the dependence on a single headend (Zein 1987). The increased initial cost over a tree topology can thus be offset by the considerable savings when only part of the network fails, rather than the whole thing.

Another factor worthy of consideration is that the technology of traditional wide area networking is not static either. When LANs were introduced in the mid 1970s, their data rates of 10 Mbit/s were many times that economically achievable on point-to-point circuit or packet switches, 64 kbit/s being considered a fast line. Now, however, packet switches can handle lines running at 1 Mbit/s, and at least one 10 Mbit/s X.25 chip is available. Thus the speed advantages of LANs are being eroded, and the cost advantages of switches — they are generally cheaper than LANs in large installations — may affect the LAN market.

It can, however, be reasonably predicted that the physical standards outlined in Part 3 will be augmented by others, with the possibility of radical changes unforeseen by ISO. It is therefore appropriate at this point to introduce one new MAC layer development, which is designed to be compatible with the ISO LLC layers. This is the *Fibre Distributed Data Interface* (FDDI), which promises to be the first OSI LAN developed specifically for fibre optic cable, and thus to restore the speed differential over wide area networks.

16.2.1   FDDI — a future fibre LAN

FDDI is being promoted by the American National Standards Institute's X3T9.5 working group, which is charged with examining high speed communications. They have concentrated on the physical and MAC layers, along with station management, choosing to model the LAN on the IEEE 802.5 token ring. There are many dissimilarities, however, the first being that there are no absolute limits on the number of stations or on the size of the ring. This will vary depending on the application, but rings of five hundred stations, spreading over 100 km, will be possible. The raw data rate of 100 Mbit/s will mean significant performance differences over current LANs.

The network is configured as two fibre rings, with the data flowing in opposite directions in the primary and the secondary circuits. In some cases both rings can be used simultaneously, but normally the secondary will only be used if the primary fails. Because it is expensive to connect each station to two rings, two classes of station have been defined. Class A stations (Fig. 16.3(a)) will be able to connect to both rings, but the simpler Class B stations (Fig. 16.3(b)) will only connect to one or other of the rings.

An extension of the Class A station, shown in Fig. 16.4, has also been defined to give the same sort of functionality as the wiring concentrator of the token ring (cf. Chapter 8). This will enable several Class B stations to be logically attached to both main rings, as the concentrator will route the traffic to whichever ring is in use. The concentrator is already being seen as

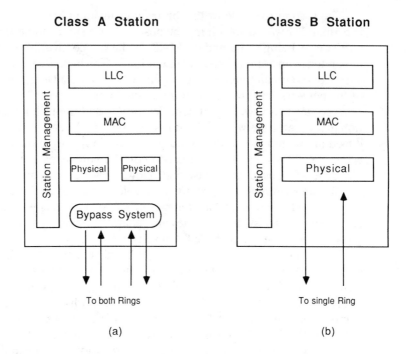

Fig. 16.3 — Class A and B FDDI station schematics.

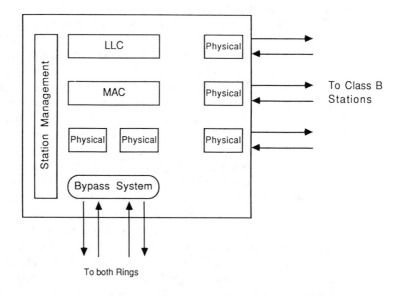

Fig. 16.4 — Class A FDDI station configured as concentrator.

enabling star or tree style topologies to be adopted, where this is more convenient than the ring.

Because of its very high speed, FDDI was originally seen as a type of *back-end* network, used to connect mainframe CPUs to fast peripherals, such as discs, usually within a computer room, or even several computer rooms many kilometres apart. As it has developed, however, it is apparent that the concentrator mechanism will permit FDDI to be used as a high speed *backbone* LAN, connecting a number of the slower ISO LANs. As all the LANs are compatible from the LLC layer upwards, and as the FDDI data rate could support traffic from several such LANs without degradation, a configuration such as that shown in Fig. 16.5 becomes a possibility.

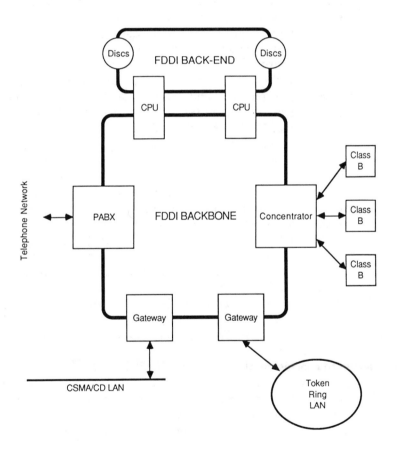

Fig. 16.5 — Example of FDDI as back-end and backbone LAN.

Fig. 16.5 also shows a PABX connected to the FDDI backbone. This is possible if the most recent work, dubbed FDDI II, is adopted. In this scheme, the 100 Mbit/s channel would be divided up into 16 channels of 6.144 Mbit/s channels, plus a control channel. As this is a convenient multiple of both the US and European voice rates, it is being pursued with great interest.

FDDI development is proceeding very quickly, with the first products already available, although the complete specification of the ANSI standard is not yet published. As this is the only fibre optic standard being promoted and as the fibre manufacturers have no entrenched positions to defend, it is likely that FDDI will be one of the fastest standards to gain widespread acceptance.

16.3   INTEGRATED SERVICES DIGITAL NETWORKS

One final aspect of standardisation must be mentioned when the future is under discussion, namely ISDN. *Integrated Service Digital Network* is a standard being developed mainly by the PTTs, to enable all communications, voice, data and video, to be transferred down a single logical cable.

At present, a large company will have separate connections to the telephone network, possibly several wide area data networks, telex, facsimile and possibly video conference networks. This results in a great deal of physical wiring, plus the complications of dealing with many network service suppliers. The idea behind ISDN is that each site will have one line to the (inter)national ISDN network, in the same way that telephones are currently on the international telephone network. Because the latest generation of telephone equipment works with digital transmission, there is no difference to the carrier between voice and data.

ISDN, however, requires an upheaval for every country, as each exchange has to be upgraded, and thus it will take many years for ISDN to become widespread. The necessary signalling standards have been defined, however, and many pilot networks exist. It may be some years before ISDN becomes relevant to LANs, as the basic local connection to a user's building is currently only rated at 64 Kbit/s. Higher speeds are part of the requirement for ISDN, however, with primary access being set at 2 Mbit/s, and some limited high speed access is possible now. Part of the UK's Alvey Project, for example, is using a 2 Mbit/s ISDN link for bridging between remotely sited LANs. This is one of the most likely future uses for ISDN, as applied to LANs.

In conclusion, it seems inevitable that computer networks will play an increasingly important role in all our lives — see for example Meek's essay 'Towards the 21st century' (Meek 1984). Local area networks will play a large part in network development, although one can expect the divisions between local and wide area networks to become increasingly blurred.

Appendix

ISO OSI standards documents

The following open systems interconnection standards documents are some of the most relevant to local area networks. They are available from the International Standards Organisation, General Secretariat, 1 Rue de Varembe, 1211 Geneva, Switzerland, or from the national standards organisations. The document number quoted is that of the service definition, with the corresponding protocol document number in parenthesis at the end of the entry. The following abbreviations are used:

ISO	Full International Standard
DIS	Draft International Standard
DP	Draft Proposal
ADD	Addendum

General

ISO 7498	Description of the Basic Reference Model for Open Systems Interconnection
DP 7498/3	Naming and Addressing
DP 9646	Conformance testing Methodology and Framework
DP 7498/4	Management Framework
DP 9595	Management Information Service (Protocol DP 9596)

Application layer

DP 9545	Application Layer Structure
DIS 8649	Common Application Service Elements (Protocol—DIS 8650)
DP 8751	File Transfer Access & Management
DP 8831	Job Transfer and Manipulation Service (Protocol—DP 8832)
DIS 9040	Virtual Terminal Basic Class Service (Protocol—DIS 9041)
DIS 8505	Functional Description and Service Specification for Message-Oriented Text Interchange Systems (MOTIS)
DIS 9065	MOTIS—Message Interchange Formats and Protocols

DIS 8883   MOTIS—Message Interchange Service and Message Transfer Protocol

ISO 7942   Graphical Kernel System (GKS)

DIS 8907   Network Database Language

Presentation layer

DIS 8822   Connection-Oriented Presentation Service (Protocol —DIS 8323)

Session layer

DIS 8326   Basic Connection-Oriented Session Service (Protocol —DIS 8327)

Transport layer

ISO 8072   Transport Service Definition
        (ADD 1 Connectionless-Mode Transmission)
        (Connection-Oriented Protocol—DIS 8073)
        (Connectionless Mode Protocol—DIS 8602)

Network layer

ISO 8348   Network Service Definition
        (ADD 1—Connectionless-Mode Transmission)
        (Connectionless Mode Protocol—DIS 8473)
        (DAD 2—Network Layer Addressing)

DIS 8878   Use of X.25 to Provide the Connection-Mode Network Service.

DP 8880   Protocol combinations to Provide and Support the Network Service

DIS 8881   Use of the X.25 Packet Level Protocol in ISO 8802 Local Area Networks

Data link and MAC layers

DIS 8886   Data Link Service Definition

DIS 8802/2   Logical Link Layer

DIS 8802/3   Local Area Networks CSMA/CD

DIS 8802/4   Local Area Networks Token Passing Bus

DIS 8802/5   Local Area Networks Token Ring

DP 8802/6   Fibre Optic Slotted Ring.

Abbreviations

ADD	ADDendum
AMP	Active Monitor Present
ANSI	American National Standards Institute
API	Applications Programming Interface
APPC	Advanced Program to Program Communications
ARPANET	Advanced Research Project Agency Network
ASCII	American Standard Code for Information Interchange
AT&T	American Telephone & Telegraph
AUI	Attachment Unit Interface
BIOS	Basic Input/Output System
BISYNC	Binary Synchronous
BIU	Bus Interface Unit
BSI	British Standards Institution
CASE	Common Application Service Elements
CATV	Community Antenna Television
CBX	Computerised Branch Exchange
CCITT	Consultative Committee on International Telegraphy & Telephony
CEN	European Committee for Standardisation
CENELEC	European Electrical Standards Co-ordinating Committee
CEPT	European Conference of Post & Telecommunications
CLIP	Connectionless Internet Protocol
CLNS	Connectionless Network Service
CNMA	Communications Network for Manufacturing Applications
CONS	Connection Oriented Network Service
CPU	Central Processing Unit
CSMA/CA	Carrier Sense Multiple Access/Collision Avoidance
CSMA/CD	Carrier Sense Multiple Access/Collision Detection
DAD	Draft Amendment Document
DARPA	Defense Advanced Research Projects Agency
DCE	Data Communications Equipment
DIS	Draft International Standard
DIU	Data Interface Unit
DIX	Digital Intel Xerox
DM	Disconnect Mode
DMA	Direct Memory Access

DOS	Disk Operating System
DOV	Data Over Voice
DP	Draft Proposal
DSAP	Destination Service Access Point
DTE	Data Terminal Equipment
ECMA	European Computer Manufacturers' Association
ECSA	Exchange Carriers Standards Association
EEC	European Economic Community (Common Market)
EN	European Norm
ENV	European Norm (Draft)
EPA	Enhanced Performance Architecture
FCS	Frame Check Sequence
FDDI	Fibre Distributed Data Interface
FDM	Frequency Division Multiplexing
FRMR	Frame Reject
FSK	Frequency Shift Keying
FTAM	File Transfer Access & Management
FTP	File Transfer Protocol
GHz	Giga-Hertz
GKS	Graphical Kernel System
GOSIP	Government Open Systems Interconnect Procurement
HDLC	High Level Data Link Control
Hz	Hertz
IBM	International Business Machines
ICMP	Internet Control Message Protocol
IEC	International Electro-technical Commission
IEE	Institution of Electrical Engineers
IEEE	Institute of Electrical and Electronic Engineers
ILD	Injection Laser Diode
IPX	Internetwork Packet eXchange
IS	International Standard
ISDN	Integrated Services Digital Network
ISO	International Standards Organisation
ISP	International Standardisation Profile
ITSU	Information Technology Standards Unit
JTMP	Job Transfer & Manipulation Protocol
Kbit/s	Kilo-bit per second
LAN	Local Area Network
LAPB	Link Access Protocol (Balanced)
LED	Light Emitting Diode
LLC	Logic Link Control
LME	Layer Management Entity
LSAP	Link Service Access Point
LU	Logical Unit
MAC	Medium Access Control
MAN	Metropolitan Area Network
MAP	Manufacturing Applications Protocol

MAU	Medium Access Unit
Mbit/s	Mega-bits per second
MHz	Mega-Hertz
MIPS	Million Instructions Per Second
MMFS	Manufacturing Message Format Standard
MMS	Manufacturing Message System
MOTIS	Message Oriented Text Interchange System
NBS	National Bureau of Standards
NCB	Network Control Block
NETBIOS	NETwork Basic Input/Output System
NFS	Network File Store
NIU	Network Interface Unit
NOS	Network Operating System
OEM	Original Equipment Manufacturer
OSI	Open Systems Interconnection
OSIRM	Open Systems Interconnection Reference Model
PABX	Private Automatic Branch eXchange
PBX	Private Branch eXchange
PC	Personal Computer
PDAD	Proposed Draft Amended Document
PDU	Protocol Data Unit
P/F	Poll/Final
POSI	Promotion conference for Open Systems Interconnection
PSK	Phase Shift Keying
PSS	Packet Switched Service
PSTN	Public Switched Telephone Network
PTT	Postal, Telegraph and Telephone
PU	Physical Unit
PVC	PolyVinyl Chloride
RAM	Random Access Memory
REJ	Frame Reject
RNR	Receiver Not Ready
ROM	Read-Only Memory
RPC	Remote Procedure Call
RR	Receiver Ready
SABME	Set Asynchronous Balanced Mode Extended
SMAP	Station Management Application Protocol
SMB	Send Message Block
SMP	Standby Monitor Present
SNA	Systems Network Architecture
SONET	Synchronous Optical NETwork
SPAG	Standards Promotion & Applications Group
SSAP	Source Service Access Point
TAG	Technical Advisory Group
TCP/IP	Transmission Control Protocol/Internet Protocol
TCU	Trunk Coupling Unit
TDM	Time Division Multiplexing

TOP	Technical and Office Protocol
UA	Unnumbered Acknowledge
UDP	User Datagram Protocol
UI	Unnumbered Information
VDU	Visual Display Unit
VLSI	Very Large Scale Integration
VTP	Virtual Terminal Protocol
WAN	Wide Area Network
WDM	Wave Division Multiplexing
XDR	eXternal Data Representation
XID	eXchange Identification
XNS	Xerox Network Service

Glossary

Address—A sequence of bytes representing the logical location of a station, or process within a station, on the network. It is usually prefixed onto the relevant "onion layer" of the protocol set.

Amplifier—A device which regenerates an analogue signal, thus increasing the distance which the signal can be sent. See Chapter 4.

Amplitude shift keying—The modulation (i.e. modifying) of a signal to carry data, by changing the amplitude (i.e. strength) of the signal to reflect the data value. See Technical Note 6 at the end of Chapter 4.

Analogue transmission—The sending of data by using a continuous signal over a medium. See Technical Note 1 at the end of Chapter 2.

Asynchronous transmission—The sending of one data character at a time, each preceded by a start bit and terminated by one or more stop bits. See Technical Note 2 at the end of Chapter 2.

Attenuation—The loss of strength of a signal as it passes through a medium. See Technical Note 3 at the end of Chapter 3.

Backup—The copying of information to provide a means of recovery from lost or corrupt data.

Bandwidth—The range of frequencies offered by a medium for the transmission of signals. Now in common usage as the data rate on a LAN. See Technical Note 3 at the end of Chapter 3.

Baseband—The transmission of a signal without modulation. In a LAN, this implies that the whole medium is used to carry one signal at a time. See Chapter 4.

Baud—A unit of measure of the rate of signal modulation. For most data purposes it is equivalent to bit/s.

Bridge—A device for linking two or more LANs which may be dissimilar at the physical layer but run the same Link Layer protocols. See Chapter 14.

Broadband—The transmission of a signal using modulation. This permits many simultaneous signals on the same medium. See Chapter 4.

Bus—A topology comprising a single linear medium to which all the stations are attached. See Chapter 4. Also the internal data path of a computer.

Byte—A set of (normally) 8 binary digits (bits).

Channel—A range of frequencies used to carry a single transmission in a Broadband network. See Chapter 4.

Checksum—An arithmetic computation on the data within a packet which is then transmitted with the packet. The receiver can then perform the same computation to determine if any data has been corrupted during transmission.

Circuit switching—The provision of a direct, dedicated, physical path between two communicating devices. See Chapter 2.

Coaxial—A type of cable comprising a solid inner conductor separated from an outer shield by a non-conducting material. See Chapter 3.

Codec—Stands for Coder/Decoder. A device for converting analogue signals to digital signals.

CSMA/CD—Carrier Sense Multiple Access with Collision Detection: a bus access technique, described in Chapter 5. See also Chapter 7.

Cyclic redundancy check—Same as Checksum.

Data circuit equipment—A device which provides a network attachment point for a user device, e.g. a modem.

Data terminal equipment—A device which acts as the origin of, or destination for, data, e.g. a computer, terminal or printer.

Datagram packet switching—The splitting up of messages into small packets, each of which is transmitted independently across the network. See Chapter 2.

Digital transmission—The sending of data using discrete signals in the medium. See Technical Note 1 at the end of Chapter 2.

Encapsulation—Enclosing a packet from one protocol by a header, and sometimes a trailer, of the next protocol down the ISO model.

Filestore—A system, usually a station on a LAN, which provides shared disc storage for the stations on the LAN.

Frame—A collection of bits grouped as one entity for transmission. Generally this refers to the packets at the Link Layer.

Frequency agile modem—A device used to connect stations to broadband networks which is capable of selecting one of several channels from which to transmit and receive data.

Frequency division multiplexing—The splitting up of a medium by frequency to enable several signals to be transmitted simultaneously. See Technical Note 5 at the end of Chapter 4.

Functional standard—A set of protocols for a given application or function, which tightly define the protocols, classes, subsets and options to be used. See Chapter 16.

Gateway—A device which links networks which run different protocols or which have different characteristics. See Chapter 14.

Headend—A piece of equipment at the 'root' of a broadband network which receives all transmissions and regenerates them to the receivers, shifting the channel frequency if required. See Chapter 4.

Host—A computer system which provides general user services over the network.

Hunt group—A collection of ports which share a common name. When called, the system selects the first free port.

Injection laser diode—An expensive high speed and high powered light source for fibre optic transmission. See Chapter 3.

Jitter—The slight changes in phase which a signal undergoes when passed round a ring without being stored and re-timed.

Light emitting diode—A relatively cheap light source for fibre optic transmission, supporting slow speeds over short distances. See Chapter 3.

Loopback—A test mechanism whereby a signal or message is reflected back to the source.

MAP—Manufacturing Applications Protocol—A set of protocols defined by General Motors for factory applications. See Chapter 16.

Message switching—The technique of sending whole messages as one entity across a network. See Chapter 2.

Modem—Modulator/Demodulator. A device for converting digital signals to analogue signals. See Chapter 4.

Multiplexing—A technique designed to carry many signals simultaneously over the same medium. See Technical Note 5 at the end of Chapter 4.

Packet—A collection of bits, including some addressing information. This is usually used to describe Network Layer entities (see Frame).

Phase shift keying—The modulation of a signal to carry data by altering the phase of the signal to reflect the value of the data. See Technical Note 6 at the end of Chapter 4.

Protocol—A set of rules governing the interchange of data between two entities. See Chapter 10.

Repeater—A device which regenerates a digital signal on a LAN, thus extending the area which a LAN can cover. See Chapter 14.

Ring—A topology where the stations are connected in a loop, with each station responsible for passing the data on to the next. See Chapter 4.

RS–232—A "standard" interface for asynchronous communications, typically found on terminals, PCs and printers.

Server—A system on the LAN which provides a service for other LAN users, e.g. a filestore or print server.

Slotted ring—A technique for access to a ring whereby an empty packet, or slot, is continuously circulating round the stations. A station may fill the slot when it receives it. See Chapter 5.

Spooling—The collection of information from several sources at one point, followed by the orderly delivery of that information to a device, e.g. a printer.

Standard—An agreed protocol governing some aspect of data interchange between systems.

Star—A topology where all of the stations are connected to a central switch. See Chapter 4.

Star-coupler—A fibre optic device which can connect several LANs into a star topology. See Chapter 7.

Switch—A device which routes data between several attached inputs and outputs.

Synchronous transmission—The sending of data in frames, i.e. blocks of data preceded by SYNC characters. See Technical Note 2 at the end of Chapter 2.

Tap—The physical attachment point to a LAN cable.

Time division multiplexing—The splitting up of a medium into time slots to permit the multiple transmission of several digital signals. See Technical Note 5 at the end of Chapter 4.

Timeout—The expiry of a given time during which some event should have occurred.

Token bus—A bus system using token ring type access methods: i.e., each station must wait for a token before transmitting. See Chapters 5 and 9.

Token ring—An access technique where a token packet travels round the ring and a station can only transmit when it has the token. See Chapters 5 and 8.

TOP—Technical Office Protocol—A set of protocols defined by Boeing for general technical and business applications. See Chapter 16.

Topology—The shape of the network, e.g. star, bus, ring or tree. See Chapter 4.

Transceiver—A device which transmits and receives signals. Usually used in reference to CSMA/CD LANs.

Tree—A topology consisting of linked bus networks, sometimes known as 'root and branch'. See Chapter 4.

Unreliable service—A protocol layer which does not guarantee to deliver packets correctly or in the correct order, for the layer above.

Virtual circuit packet switching—The technique of providing a *logical* path between two communicating systems, along which packets are transmitted.

Windowing—The technique of permitting a transmitter to send a number of packets in advance of receiving acknowledgments for packets already sent. See Chapter 11.

X.25—A protocol defined by CCITT for use between systems. This is used in the B.T. PSS network.

Trademarks

The following are believed to be trademarks and are acknowledged as such.

ARCNET	Datapoint Corporation
DR-NET	Digital Research
Ethernet	Digital Equipment Corp., Intel & Xerox
HINET	Apricot Computers
IBM, PC-Network, NETBIOS, Netview	International Business Machines
INFAPLUG	INFA Communications
LAN/PC	Interactive Systems (3M)
MS-Net, MS-DOS, Redirector	Microsoft Corp.
Netware, Advanced Netware	Novell
UNIX	A.T. & T. (Bell Laboratories)

References

Abraham, M. (1986) Running Ethernet modems over broadband cable *Data Communications* **15**, 5 199–212.

Andrews, D. and Shultz, G. (1982) A token ring architecture for local area networks. *Proceedings of 25th IEEE Computer Society Conference.* pp. 615–624.

Bates, R. & Abramson, P. (1986) You can use phone wire for your token ring LAN. *Data Communications* **15**, 12 223–229.

Berman, C. (1986) Data over voice. *Communications* **3**, 12 17–18.

Borsook, P. (1987) TCP/IP and interoperability—separating myth from reality *Data Communications* **16**, 10 60–62.

Burg, F. & Chen, C. (1984) Of local networks, protocols and the OSI reference model. *Data Communications* **13**, 13 129–150.

Cole, M. (1982) Cambridge ring—European developments. *Local Networks & Distributed Systems* Vol 2.

Colvine, A. (1983) CSMA with collision avoidance. *Computer Communications* **6**, 5 227–235.

Currie, S. (1986) *The LAN jungle book.* Edinburgh Regional Computing Centre.

Deasington, R. (1984) *A practical guide to computer communications and networking.* Ellis Horwood.

Deasington, R. (1986) *X.25 explained.* Ellis Horwood.

Dixon, R. (1982) Ring network topology for local communications. *Proceedings, of 25th IEEE Computer Society Conference.* 591–605.

ECMA-97 (1985) *Local area networks safety requirements.* European Computer Manufacturers Association.

Gilmore, B. (1985) An appraisal of the advantages and disadvantages of using a PABX for data traffic. *Proceedings of Networks '85* 195–211.

Henshall, J. & Shaw, A. (1988) *ISO/OSI explained.* Ellis Horwood.

Howe, C. (1987) Manhunt for missing link: 10 Mbit/s Ethernet via phone wire. *Data Communications* **16**, 4 54–56.

Hurwitz, M. (1985) MS-DOS 3.1 Makes it easy to use IBM PCs on a network. *Data Communications* **14**, 12 223–237.

IEEE (1986) Draft IEEE Standard 802.1: Part D MAC Bridges. Institute of Electrical and Electronic Engineers.

IEEE (1987) Draft IEEE Standard 802.1: Overview, interworking and system management. Institute of Electrical and Electronic Engineers.

Institute of Electrical Engineering (1986) Worldwide standardisation activities on open systems interconnect and local area networks.

International Data Corporation (1986) Lan survey report.

Internet Protocol (1981) U.S. Military Standard 1777. SRI International.

James, M. (1987) Keeping hands on power. *The Guardian*, 26th March 1987.

Leong, J. (1985) Nuts and bolts guide to Ethernet installation and interconnection. *Data Communications* **14**, 10 267–276.

MAP 2.1 (1985) Manufacturing Automation Protocol Specification 2.1. General Motors Technical Centre.

Markov, J. & Strole, N. (1982) Token ring local area networks: a perspective *Proceedings of 25th IEEE Computer Society Conference* 606–614.

Meek, B. (1984) Towards the 21st century. Essay in *New Information Technology*, editor Alan Burns, Ellis Horwood.

Meir, E. (1986) Question: how open is IBM's much touted token ring? *Data Communications* **15**, 1 47–52.

Metcalf, R. & Boggs, D. (1976) Ethernet: distributed packet switching for local computer networks. *Communications of the ACM* **19**, 7 395–403.

Padlipsky, M. (1985) *The elements of networking style*. Prentice Hall.

Pape, A. (1983) The office of the future—some sociological perspectives on office work and office technology. *Computerisation of Working Life*, Ellis Horwood.

PC News (1986) U.S. Survey reports, November and December.

PC Week (1986–A) Report on *Financial Times* Professional PC Conference.

PC Week (1986–B) Report on PC Networking Conference (Microsoft, Olivetti and 3-Com).

PC Week (1987) Report on a Survey of U.S. Corporate Users.

Rankine, L. (1986) A view from the International Organisation for Standards. (Keynote address to the 8th International Conference on Computer Communications, Munich 1986). *Computer Networks & ISDN Systems* 12.

Rose, M. & Cass, D. (1987) OSI Transport services on top of the TCP, *Computer Networks and ISDN Systems* 12 159–173.

Routt, T. (1987) SNA & OSI: IBM building upper layer gateways. *Data Communications* **16**, 4 120–142.

Rudin, H. (1986) Trends in Computer Communications, *IEEE Computer* **19**, 10 25–33.

Shipp, W. & Webber, H. (1982) The Brown University network—BRUNET. *Proceedings of 25th IEEE Computer Society Conference*, 255–261.

Stallings, W. (1984) *Local networks*, MacMillan.

Stieglitz, M. (1985) IBM provides industry with a versatile local network, standard. *Data Communications* **14**, 6 195–206.

Strauss, P. (1987) OSI throughput performance: Breakthrough or bottleneck? *Data Communications* **16**, 4 53–56.

Tanenbaum, A. (1981) *Computer Networks*, Prentice Hall.

TOP (1985) Technical and office protocol. Boeing Computer Services.

Transmission Control Protocol (1981) U.S. Military Standard 1781. SRI International.

Zein, A. (1987) Doing a broadband MAP LAN? Star far outshines tree. *Data Communications* **16**, 4 60–62.

Index

Commonly used mnemonics are used in the index — their expanded forms can be found in the abbreviations section. Bold numbers indicate the main entry in the text.

ELLIS HORWOOD BOOKS IN COMPUTING SCIENCE
General Editors: Professor JOHN CAMPBELL, University College London, and BRIAN L. MEEK, King's College London (KQC), University of London
Series in Computers and Their Applications
Series Editor: BRIAN L. MEEK, Computer Centre, King's College London (KQC), University of London